ATTACK AND DEFENCE

A History of RAF Langham and its Dome Trainer

To Tony
Best Wishes

Mick Barked.

LANGHAM DOME

Small building. big story!

ATTACK AND DEFENCE

A History of RAF Langham and its Dome Trainer

Mick Barham & Mark Glaister

Dedication

To those who gave their lives and especially those lost but never found

ISBN 978 1 90387 242 0

British Library Cataloguing in Publication Data
A catalogue record for this book is available from the British Library

First published 2024
Produced and published by Posthouse Publishing, No 2 Cleat,
St Margaret's Hope, South Ronaldsay, Orkney, KW17 2RW
www.posthousepublishing.com

Printed in Great Britain

About the Authors

Mick Barham and Mark Glaister are joint archivists at The Langham Dome Museum, entertaining visitors to the Dome for the past number of years with stories of vision, ingenuity, bravery, endurance and sacrifice that they have collected over time – and still discover today. Here they have committed many of those stories to print both as a memento of a visit to the Dome and to introduce RAF Langham to a wider audience.

CONTENTS

Foreword by
The Lord Dannatt GCB CBE MC

Attack and Defence, as the title describes, is a story about the heroic and often tragic attack sorties by aircraft flying from the wartime RAF Langham, and the defensive skills being honed, to save lives, within the anti-aircraft training dome on the airbase – in a rural corner of North Norfolk. Before the Second World War and now, Langham is a quiet agricultural village but behind the tranquillity of pastoral life is a fiercely proud episode. This little local community hosted one of the key hubs of action that played a major role in ridding Europe of tyranny and returning values of peace and freedom to the people of the United Kingdom and of Europe.

This story is about an airbase, the aeroplanes that flew from there and the air defence training that went on, but first and foremost it is a story about people. The local folk of Langham provide the backdrop but on to the stage came men and women in the distinctive uniforms of the Royal Air Force, and later in the uniforms of Allied air forces. Flying half way around the world came 455 Squadron of the Royal Australian Air Force and 489 Squadron of the Royal New Zealand Air Force, forming a strong bond with Langham, sadly forty-seven members of these squadrons made the ultimate sacrifice. But all these incredible people came with their hopes and fears, their nervousness and their confidence, their ambitions and their determination. The noise of aero engines pierced the huge Norfolk skies by day and by night as the fight was carried to the enemy while in the Langham Dome special skills were being taught to protect our citizens from hostile assault.

Today, the RAF Langham airfield has gone, but like so much of East Anglia, which was a giant patchwork of wartime airbases, what you cannot fail to notice from the air is that an airfield was there, but what remains for all to see on the ground is the Langham Dome. In the rush to return the airfield to civilian and economic use, the Dome seemed to be overlooked. For years it gradually decayed and could have suffered the eventual fate of the many defensive pillboxes scattered around the English countryside. But the Dome represented a challenge to which the people of Langham have risen.

What could have remained an anonymous derelict building has now been transformed into not just a replica of its original wartime purpose but also into a fascinating museum that holds the spirit and the story of those dark days in the 1940's and the return of hope in the 1950's. In this compelling book, local archivists, Mick Barham and Mark Glaister, have put into print many of the stories with which they have enthralled visitors since the Langham Dome was refurbished and opened to the public on 19th July 2014. Now enriched by a World

War 2 Spitfire aircraft, a visit to the Langham Dome is a day to remember – and an opportunity to reflect with gratitude on the service and sacrifice of those who served and flew from RAF Langham, many never to return. The refurbished Langham Dome itself is a testament to the dedication of local people who have worked so hard to keep this important chapter of our history alive. Readers will enjoy this book, visitors to the Langham Dome will have a memorable day and all associated with the refurbishment project are to be warmly congratulated.

Preface

The main idea for this book is to provide visitors to the Langham Dome with a reminder of their visit. However, we also recognised a need to preserve, we hope for those interested, a short history of events that surround The Dome and its associated airfield, RAF Langham. For the visitor, we wanted to offer a more in-depth account of the two key themes of the museum – the Dome Trainer and RAF Langham – to be studied by the visitor at leisure.

Divided into two main sections that equally represent these themes, each part is further divided into chapters that provide contextual, biographical, factual and operational details in a contemporaneous, sequential order – the idea being that it

will hopefully satisfy a wide range of readers, in that it can be followed either in the form of a 'story' from cover to cover, or used as an occasional reference piece to seek out relevant sections according to specific interests. We hope we have managed to strike the right balance between narrative and technical detail in satisfying all readers' reasons for picking up this small tome and not allowed our enthusiasm as volunteers and archivists at The Dome to let us get carried away.

We uncover new stories connected with the Museum all the time. There are so many compelling accounts that have presented themselves that it was always a challenge while compiling the book deciding what went in and what stayed out. Some emerged during the course of writing, which made the choices even more difficult. We have tried to select the best cross-section of narratives from the ordinary to the extraordinary. None, however, not even those omitted, is mundane. Every one has a tale to tell and our aim in the Museum is to keep them all alive for our visitors. We hope our selection here at least is satisfactory.

Inevitably in such a book as this, our efforts rest on the shoulders of others' former labour and success. The predecessor to this publication, *R.A.F Langham 1940-1958: a Brief History*, was largely the work of the late Len Bartram. For Part II of this book, we have leaned heavily on his extensive research. Ewan Ward-Thomas, Henry Stephens's grandson, gave us unstinting access to all manner of documents allowing us to fill in some of the finer points of Henry's life. Thanks to Malcolm English for generously donating his time and expertise in proof reading. We are particularly indebted to Patrick Allen, the Chair of Trustees, for his constant collaboration and encouragement from the very early days of this project right through to publication. Without his support, this book would never have made the light of day. Enormous thanks to Peter van Stigt, who not only granted us permission to use his stunning image for the book cover but generously donated it free of charge.

Finally, we would like to dedicate this book to our friends at Langham Dome (they know who they are) for their support and encouragement and making our time there such a pleasure but most of all to our brilliant, forbearing wives, Sue and Grace, both of whom have tolerated the endless hours of the two of us locked together producing this little volume.

Mick Barham and Mark Glaister, Holt, Norfolk 2024

List of Illustrations

In The Beginning

"What are you going to do about that?" The voice came from across the forecourt.

It was May 1997 and the question was posed by the eminent local architect, Sir Bernard Feilden. It was directed at Patrick Allen, Chairman of Langham Parish Council, who had been pondering over that very point with another man, who represented the landowners.

Looking round, Patrick replied: "We're not really sure."

They were on a stretch of concrete by the side of the road between the villages of Langham and Cockthorpe looking at an incongruous, oddly-domed and deserted structure apparently in the middle of nowhere.

"It's a listed building. An official Ancient Monument in fact." Patrick explained.

"Well, it can't be left like that."

"I agree, but what's to be done about it?"

After some discussion about the lack of money needed for any preservation, Sir Bernard said he had an idea where there may be some help. Little did either of them realise that it would take the next twenty years to bring the building back to life.

And so it was that in January 2010, the local community of Langham, a quiet, picturesque, rural village in North Norfolk, came together to rescue The Dome from disrepair. It turned out to have quite a story.

To set about restoring this strange building, those few dedicated people set up the Friends of Langham Dome in order to work with the construction's owners, North Norfolk Historic Buildings Trust, who in turn had had it donated to them by Bernard Matthews plc, the owners of the land on which it stood.

In the early days, there was a deal of work carried out by various parties in trying to establish the Dome's original use, taking them down plenty of blind alleys. Several suggested that it had been a Torpedo Attack Trainer. Others argued that it had been an Astrodome for the training of navigators in night navigation. Eventually the Friends discovered it was in fact an anti-aircraft gunnery trainer, the invention of a far-sighted ex-naval officer, Henry Stephens, and had saved the Allies precious millions of pounds and, more importantly, probably countless lives.

The significance of this little structure grew as the Friends discovered more about it. Of the forty-six permanent concrete and steel Domes that were built for the RAF in this country, there were only six left standing and all of them in a state of dilapidation. So, if the Langham Dome example could be restored, it would represent a unique corner of history.

And there was more. In years gone by it wasn't in the middle

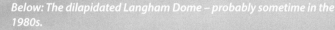

of nowhere. It was also the site of what was RAF Langham – a busy operational airfield throughout the Second World War and the early 'Cold War' period. The base and the building had seen great changes and many personnel come and go during its heyday.

As we now know, this special building was indeed restored and is now open to the public and schools telling the story of Langham's Dome and the important contribution made by the Dome Trainers in the defence of this country during the Second World War, as well as the history of RAF Langham itself. The Spitfire mounted outside is also a memorial to those that served at Langham and particularly those that flew from the airfield and never made it back.

This is the exceptional story of RAF Langham, its remarkable people and the truly extraordinary Dome.

Part I: The Dome

1. Setting the Scene

By 1918, the aeroplane had shown its potential in war. It was also clear that, with advances in aircraft design and technology progressing with each ensuing year, this potential would grow significantly. In the same way, ground- and ship-based anti-aircraft gunnery would be essential for the protection and defence of military and civilian targets against air attack.

Whilst the prospective weapons required for anti-aircraft (A-A) defence were in existence, effective A-A gunnery skills and training were not. Authorities did not always see the need. Air attack in the 1914-18 conflict was somewhat haphazard – the early 'bombers' entailed the pilot grabbing hold of a bomb from inside the cockpit and dropping it by hand over the side! The first air raids on Britain were accomplished by slow-moving Zeppelins. But that was about to change.

As the 1930s heralded the rise of Nazi Germany and its aggressive expansion across Europe, that promise of aircraft advancement and its consequential impact was being realised on an unprecedented scale. Air attack had now proven itself to be a devasting weapon. The crushing and overwhelming *Blitzkrieg* strategy executed by the German Forces in their rapid occupation of most of Europe was in large part owing to the terrifying, destructive power of the air attacks that preceded the infantry advance.

In the late 1930s, Britain was perilously unprepared for war. The initial period of the war, the 'Phoney War' as it became known, where little of any consequence seemed to be happening, did not help. The retreat to Dunkirk saw the British Expeditionary Force (BEF) having to abandon most of its weaponry in France including light A-A guns. The consequential scarcity of A-A weaponry meant that few were available for A-A training.

With the attention of Goering's Luftwaffe about to turn to her shores, Britain found the war was suddenly and profoundly on its doorstep. The prospects looked bleak. One man's vision, however, was about to offer an extraordinary lifeline.

2. Henry Stephens's life and vision

It's a remarkable thing to observe that Dome Trainers, first conceived in the 1940s, are still in use today. It's also true to say, then, that the man, whose far-sighted idea it was, must have been quite remarkable too. So, what do we know of Henry Christian Stephens?

Born in December 1896 into a reasonably well-to-do

Right: German Do217 bombers heading out on another raid.

Period advertisement for Stephens' Ink.

family (part of the dynasty that established the Stephens' Ink Company[1]), living at Grove House, Church End Finchley. At the time of his birth, Henry already had six brothers and one sister, a younger sister would come along in 1898. So, life had begun well for Henry, and his prospects for the future seemed distinctly promising. Sadly, even for one so young, misfortune was stalking in the wings.

In 1899, when Henry was just two years old their father, Julian, died. The loss of the head of the household dealt a serious blow to the family and especially to the children's mother, Minna. However, by 1901, the family seemed to have recovered and moved to 37, Compayne Gardens, Hampstead, a large house with a domestic staff of six. But tragedy struck another dreadful blow when Minna too died, just three years after her husband. The loss of both parents in such a short space of time must have been devastating for Henry, now aged five, and his siblings. Even with support and shelter from the wider family, particularly their uncle (Minna's younger brother, Michael), the next few years would have been a constant struggle for them.

But life, albeit difficult under these circumstances, had to go on. Amongst other things, their new guardians focused on the priority concern, particularly in the case of the seven boys, namely securing suitable future professions and careers.

All this would, of course, be consistent with the thinking and expectation of families of similar social status in those late-Victorian times, which was a very different prospect from what we would understand today in terms of education or training.

For young Henry, the road led to the sea and the Royal Navy – a prestigious career in those days. Britannia really did rule the waves at that time, with the largest, most formidable fleet in the world. After completing basic schooling, he entered the Incorporated Thames Nautical Training College in 1908, aged just 11 years.

Housed on *HMS Worcester II* (formerly Royal Navy ship *HMS*

Frederick William, a sail and steam-propelled ship moored on the Thames at Greenhithe), the overall objective of the college was to train potential officer material for service with either the Merchant or Royal Navy. Registered as a cadet pupil, Henry was to be resident on board for the duration of his training.

In line with *Worcester's* objective of producing officers who could "navigate around the world", Henry and his fellow cadets began their day with some 4 to 5 hours of schooling, taught by a team of masters responsible to the Headmaster, Mr David Beatty. Lessons focused on navigation, nautical astronomy and world geography. The rest of the day was given over to hands-on technical training covering all aspects of practical seamanship.

Juxtaposed with the more scholarly studies, was the seamanship and boat work training for both sail and steam. The teaching of boat work fell to the Technical Instructors, all ex-naval Petty Officers. Under their guidance, Henry and the other fresh-faced cadets embarked on lengthy practical learning, covering the essentials of best drill, sail drill, quad drill, rifle drill, knots, bends and hitches, sail making, signalling and lead line work. The days were full and, once fed and watered at supper, the young cadets were soon slumbering soundly in their hammocks.

Right: HMS Worcester II.

It wasn't all work. Sport was also catered for. At weekends, particularly Saturday afternoons, cadets could be seen playing football, cricket and tennis matches on a field in Greenhithe, all adding to the benefit of the frequent core P.E. elements of rowing and swimming.

At 15 years old, his next step was honing his skills in preparation for his forthcoming role as Junior Midshipman. Henry did his time. At last, arrival onboard his first posting:

Name: Stephens, H.C.; age: 16; rank: Probationary Midshipman; post: *HMS Hibernia*, RN Battleship.

It was September 1913. One year later and his world was about to change beyond anything he could have imagined.

As Henry was making his way in life, events in wider Europe were undergoing a series of increasingly ominous turns. The point of ignition came on 28th June 1914, when the Archduke Franz Ferdinand, heir to the Austro-Hungarian throne, was assassinated together with his wife Sophie, by a young Bosnian Serb, Gavrilo Princep, during an ill-advised visit to Sarajevo. The dominoes began to fall.

On 28th July, prompted and manipulated by Germany, Austria-Hungary declared war on Serbia. First Russia came to Serbia's defence. In turn, the alliance with Austria-Hungary drew in Germany. France and Britain, along with their respective colonies, soon followed in opposition to Germany's aggressive manoeuvrings. Outright war was declared on 4th August. By November, the Ottoman Empire joined Germany and Austria-Hungary and formed the Central Powers. Britain, France, Russia and Serbia stood against them with Italy switching sides in April 1915. The war to end all wars was underway.

During 1914 and most of 1915, *Hibernia* and her sister ships frequently put to sea. All in all though, *Hibernia* saw no main action. It was late October 1915 that a new Sub-Lieutenant, Guy Phelips, joined the ship's company. Now a full Midshipman, Henry encountered Phelips daily. From the outset the two saw eye to eye and, before long, struck up what proved to be a lifelong friendship. It was also one that years later had a profound bearing on our story.

Late in 1915, Henry had his first taste of action in the Gallipoli Campaign. It was not to be his last. After a period of leave, he received a new posting: *HMS Milbrook* a newly built 'M-class' Destroyer. He reported for duty in late February 1916. Some three months later, more battle experience came his way in spectacular fashion. The Battle of Jutland proved to be the largest, most notorious naval battle of the war. There were significant losses on both sides, but the *Milbrook* and Henry emerged unscathed.

Henry's service on *Milbrook* came to an end in early October

1916. His next posting was *HMS Columbella*, an armed Merchant Navy cruiser carrying out convoy protection and associated duties on the Northern Patrol. During his time on *Columbella*, Henry was promoted to Sub-Lieutenant. He went on to serve on two more ships, *HMS Alsation* and *HMS Arrogant*. By the later part of 1918, Germany was on the brink of defeat. In November, just before the Armistice was signed, he received notification that he was to be discharged from Navy service. As 1919 came around, aged just 22, he was back in 'civvy street' with his extended family in Finchley.

So, what to do? Henry needed a new career, a new direction. By one means or another, he took up photography as his new profession. This proved to be a good choice. After showing a deal of promise, Henry was taken on as a press photographer by the Daily Mail newspaper. His life beyond the Navy was looking up. Conditions in post-war Britain though were difficult. Prime Minister Lloyd George's promise of a "land fit for heroes" soon give way to problems and unrest. There was plenty for the press to report and Henry was kept busy gaining valuable experience and sharpening the skills of his new trade.

It was at this time Henry met his future wife. Elizabeth was significantly older than he and had already been married with an 11-year-old daughter, Phyllis. Henry and Elizabeth married in October 1920 and by 3rd July 1926, they had a daughter of their own, Evelyn Bridget Patricia. Henry's career as a press photographer was going well, and, by 1930, he was established in a consultancy role. Now things were really looking good, and the future promised much. There was, of course, just the matter of fate and world history waiting in the wings to impact Henry's life once more.

While Henry's life and work progressed through to the early to mid-1930s, events on the European stage were once more gaining perilous momentum. Adolf Hitler's Nazis had come to power on a platform of anti-communism and ultra-nationalism and, almost by default, Hitler found himself appointed Chancellor. Through the use of violence, threat and devious backroom alliances, Hitler manoeuvred his position until, in August 1934, he declared himself absolute Fuhrer.

Now fully empowered, on 7th March 1936, he ordered an invasion of the demilitarised Rhineland territory. Two years later, on 12th March 1938, he ordered his forces into Austria and annexed the territory in the so-called *Anschluss*. It did not stop there. On 17th September, Germany also annexed the Sudetenland (the northern, southern and western areas of Czechoslovakia). All this was on the pretext of uniting the Germanic populaces.

In the face of this, the British Government, a coalition led by the Prime Minister Neville Chamberlain, pursued a policy

of appeasement. With the hope of avoiding another world war, they acquiesced to Hitler's pretext. This culminated in the Munich Agreement, signed on 30th September 1938, by Britain, France and Italy on the one hand and Germany on the other. Chamberlain believed it would deliver "peace in our time". As it turned out, time was the only thing gained.

Henry had already experienced the potential consequences of such aggression. Despite this, he and Elizabeth were getting on with life as much as possible, including trips to the cinema in Leicester Square, close to their flat in Charing Cross Road. One of their visits would prove to embrace a pivotal moment.

As was commonplace in the late 1930s, the programme that evening included a newsreel from Pathé News. For most people, the cinema was the only place at the time where they could watch the news in moving pictures. This particular news bulletin showed German Ju87 'Stuka' dive bombers carrying out attacks in the Spanish Civil War which had been raging since July 1936. Henry was utterly shaken by what he saw. This was a world away from his experience of war in the previous conflict. Here, in the hands of the Nazis, was an altogether new, fearsome machine – totally different from anything

Left: German Junkers Ju87 Stuka dive bombers making their menacing debut in the Spanish Civil War.

in the First World War – wreaking havoc and obliteration in sudden, brief and unprecedented attacks. Being ex-Navy, his thoughts immediately turned to ships at sea. It was at this moment Henry realised, as it stood, if Britain were to go to war again, Navy gunners were simply not sufficiently trained, experienced or suitably equipped to defend against this potentially devastating weapon. Britannia might have hitherto ruled the waves, but the Royal Navy, as powerful and predominant as it was, would likely be overwhelmed.

Henry's fears were to be realised all too soon. On 15th March 1939, Hitler invaded the remaining territories of Czechoslovakia and a few weeks later occupied regions of Lithuania. In May, Germany and Italy joined forces in a political and military pact. But Hitler had another devious trick up his sleeve that spelt the death knell for Europe. With false promises of equally dividing up any future occupied territories of Eastern Europe, Hitler signed a 'non-aggression pact' with the Soviet Union. This meant any potential threat Germany might face from the Soviets in the East was neutralised. The only potential enemies Hitler might face were now entirely to the West.

Unhindered, Hitler now stepped up the pace and executed his plans to overthrow Europe. On 1st September, he ordered the invasion of Poland in direct contravention of the Munich Agreement. It was now clear Hitler's ambitions extended far beyond the unification of Germany and its people. Having given guarantees of support for Poland, Britain stated in an ultimatum note to Germany on 3rd September 1944 that it would "fulfil its obligations to Poland". With no response offered by the German government to this and a subsequent final note, at 11.15am, the British Prime Minister, Neville Chamberlain made his now historic announcement on BBC Home Service. On 4th September the BEF, commanded by Lord Gort, began crossing the Channel into France.

Not realising it at the time, Henry's moment had come.

3. The Dome Trainer Comes to Life

Little did he know at the time, but Henry was about to devise the first truly successful virtual reality system. It's a concept that we're quite familiar with in today's world where so much is based on digital media but consider for a moment what that meant in a predominantly analogue world. It's genuinely amazing to realise that someone, from a time so far before computers being commonplace, could turn such a notion into reality. And realism is the key word here. Back in war-torn 1940s Britain, it was a truly extraordinary leap forward.

So, let's briefly take a look at that era. What was the state of A-A defence training before the Dome Trainer?

At the time of the First World War, there had been a gradual recognition that perhaps establishing an anti-aircraft defence would be a sensible resource. Britain began by forming A-A sections within the Army to support the BEF in France. Progress was slow with only a few units reaching France by September 1914. Matters improved during and after 1915, but the fact remained that, right up to the war's end, Britain's A-A effectiveness continued to suffer from a number of shortcomings. Weaponry was top of the list. There was no development of a single dedicated A-A weapon. What was available was adapted from existing weapons. Added to this was the issue of inadequate training which, owing to the nature of the rather makeshift approach to weaponry, was rather haphazard and largely based on trial and error.

Between the wars there was some attempt to improve technical aspects of gunnery skills. For example, the Army's 1931 Small Arms Manual, which covered everything from pistols to machine guns, had a brief section on anti-aircraft techniques. The text goes into detail about what instructors should teach the trainees on the fitting and use of an 'A-A aim corrector' (a very unsophisticated gunsight to offset aim that made no allowance for speed of the target aircraft), the correct stance for the gunner to take and 'rules of aiming' depending on whether the attacking aircraft is diving, climbing or

Right: One of the better pre-war methods of anti-aircraft training, still critically lacking the sophistication of Dome Trainers.

crossing. Some rules were to be "taught by diagram". The practical sessions entailed aiming at a model aeroplane on a pole!

Still the inertia surrounding A-A defence continued. It took until 1938 for a dedicated Anti-Aircraft Command to be established and with it the 1st and 2nd A-A Divisions created. By the outbreak of the Second World War, seven A-A Divisions were in place. But training issues persisted. There were at least now classroom-based instruction for these units, however hands-on A-A aiming and firing practice remained quite basic. For example, sometime during 1940/41, Charles Bell, then a Navy Gunnery School Instructor based in North Wales, sought to improve practical 'aim-off training' via use of 'target' aircraft models pulled along an elevated wire. A step in the right direction at least, but still a long way from bridging the gap between practice and reality.

Some training was perhaps able to achieve a measure of live ammunition aiming and firing practice when the Anti-Aircraft Cooperation Units began target towing operations in the late 1930s, but this was using relatively slow-moving linear flag banner/drogue sleeve targets, scant preparation for defending against dive bombing and other forms of aerial attack. A parlous situation that would persist right through to 1942 and Henry's Dome Trainer.

It was the lack of realistic attack scenarios where these and other existing training practices and systems fell short. They simply did not – and could not – address the wide variety of attack profiles and configurations of the faster, more manoeuvrable aircraft that were by then in existence. Moreover, they did not incorporate any of the associated skills with air defence, such as understanding the different operational functions of the variety of enemy aircraft types. This would involve identifying the aircraft type as you take aim, so recognising that a dive bomber will behave in a totally different way to a ground attack fighter and yet again from a medium bomber. If they could develop these kinds of expertise, it would mean the A-A gunners were thereby given a slight advantage in expecting what the aircraft attack profile would be. In plain terms, they would know what the pilot would likely do next and be ready to fire at the best possible moment to score hits. Model aircraft on wires and target tugs simply did not offer this option.

So, when war did come in September 1939, Britain was not only short of A-A weapons – it had, for the most part, only machine guns to defend airfields and other potential low-level attack targets – but also gunners who had little to no appropriate practical aiming and firing drilling against the enemy aircraft types and attack patterns they were soon to encounter. It is fair to say that, outside the 'silent classroom', such training for those gunners involved, for the most part,

RAF Volunteer Reserve recruits running around parts of the field with pole-mounted model aircraft, to provide targets for them to practice aiming-off!

Thankfully that was about to change as Henry's solution totally transformed training in thoroughly preparing these fighting men for what they would face in a real air attack.

Over the weeks and months following Chamberlain's sombre radio broadcast and with the grim exigencies of war now a part of daily life, like the rest of the country, Henry followed news of the war's progress. Those stark images of the 'Stukas' in the newsreel came back into sharp focus again. His mind ran on. Navy gunners were going to need specific training in defensive firing against aerial attacks, particularly dive bombing. Could he possibly help? As he pondered the situation, an embryo of an idea began to form – a training system for anti-aircraft gunners. He envisaged realistic, moving images of attacking aircraft, projected onto a curved screen of some sort, just as they would appear to anti-aircraft gunners onboard ship.

As 1939 gave way to 1940, Henry devoted more and more thought as to how his idea would work in practice. His spare time was taken up as he worked on key elements of his concept. His head filled with cine cameras, aircraft, film and projector speeds and a myriad of other details. He pressed on for several months until his idea was suitably firmed up.

Happy with his progress, Henry was nevertheless aware that he had reached the point where he needed to involve the military to bring his scheme into being. Who could he turn to? The answer was a simple one. He would approach his old friend and former shipmate, Guy Phelips, still in the Navy as a Lieutenant Commander in charge of the Photographic School at Tipnor. Thinking back to their experiences on *HMS Hibernia* at the time of the First World War, Henry was in no doubt. Guy was the perfect choice.

Henry wasted no time in getting in touch with Phelips. He explained the idea of using a cine camera to film British aircraft simulating different forms of aerial attack by enemy aeroplanes and how the images obtained would then be projected onto the internal walls of a dome. He described how the projector would move in the same 'panning track' as the original cine camera so that the apparent size and speed of the aircraft images would be exactly as experienced during a real enemy aircraft attack.

Guy took it all in as Henry went on to outline details for long-and short-range A-A gunnery training, including analysis of aim by projecting a spot of light onto the dome surface to show the correct aiming point required to hit the moving aircraft. He also covered the notion of using loudspeaker sound effects of dive bombing and other short-range attacks, including machine gun fire, to match the film being played, thus making the training as realistic as possible so that the trainees would become used to these battle sounds.

With the ideas already so well developed, Phelips was convinced that Henry had hit on something of vital importance and advised his best course of action was to re-join the Navy. Henry was by this time 43, so Phelips suggested the Royal Navy Volunteer Reserve (RNVR) and to expedite matters, wrote a private letter to his friend and Navy contact Commander Weekes, serving on the Admiralty staff of a Second Sea Lord covering personnel, recruiting, training bases and facilities. In a matter of days, Henry was offered an interview and on 8th July 1940, he was appointed as temporary Sub-Lieutenant, RNVR to the authorities at the RN College, Greenwich. A new and exciting chapter of his life was about to begin.

During his first week at Greenwich, Henry wrote a brief 'letter summary' to the College Commander, J. Doyley, outlining his basic proposal for the 'Dome A-A Teacher'. Doyley forwarded this to the College President, Captain J.C. Davis, who granted Henry an audience. After hearing Henry elaborate, Davis appreciated that he may be onto something but still wanted to establish that the scheme was technically feasible. So, Davis removed Henry from 'normal duties' and attached him to Lieutenant Commander Pigou (who also happened to be Henry's brother-in-law, married to Henry's elder sister Agnes). The pair were instructed to consult photographic and cinematographic experts to discuss and confirm the viability of specific aspects of Henry's idea without, in the interests of secrecy, revealing full details of the scheme.

Not even a month after Henry had re-joined the Navy, he was already meeting one of the first experts on their list, a Mr Warmisham of Taylor, Taylor and Hobson Ltd., manufacturing opticians and engineers. Warmisham was a well-established specialist on cinematographic lenses. He not only confirmed the practicability of several optical elements of Henry's idea but went further, suggesting a meeting with Technicolor Ltd., who he was confident could deliver the accuracy required for the aircraft films.

This was an excellent start, but Henry hardly had time to draw breath before Pigou whisked him off a few days later to visit Commander Campbell at the Anti-Aircraft department of *HMS Excellent*, the Navy's Gunnery School down at Whale Island, Portsmouth. Campbell too reacted favourably to Henry's proposal, rating its potential as being "of the highest value". So much so that he took Henry and Pigou to the Naval Anti-Aircraft School at nearby Eastney, to show them some equipment used to record naval gun movements. Campbell explained how this gear could be adapted to record cine camera movements when filming real aircraft for use in Henry's Dome Teacher. This came as an ideal vindication for

Henry as he had already highlighted issues with Pigou, Phelips and Davis on the need for recording camera movements.

Pigou and Henry met Mr Warmisham again the next day, together with Mr W. Oliver of Technicolor, to discuss various details of Henry's scheme. Five days later, on 12th August 1940, Henry and Oliver visited the Navy's Gunnery School at Chatham to inspect more existing equipment that Oliver believed could be used to move projectors and take photographs.

With the feedback reaching Captain Davis from these meetings so positive, Henry was asked to commit a more in-depth summary to paper. On 14th August, he submitted a detailed four-page 'letter report' addressed to Davis. Beyond the introduction, Henry's report covered proposals for filming, a description of operations in the dome, the methodologies for both long- and short-range training (following Pigou's advice on the corresponding differences in gunnery techniques) and suggested the use of soundtracks to add to the realism. The report also proposed a wood frame and canvas construction for an experimental dome. Henry had clearly done his thinking since all the key elements that we now see in the Dome facility today were already developing in his mind.

There was no let-up in pace. On 24th August, Captain Brind, the officer in charge of *HMS Excellent*, sent a report on the 'Dome Teacher' scheme to Admiral Sir William James, the Commander-in-Chief at Portsmouth, with recommendations that "steps now be taken" to start the project. By 27th August, Admiral James had forwarded Brind's report to the Admiralty, under a covering letter containing the wording:

"Forwarded for the early consideration of Their Lordships and recommending that formalities be dispensed with and Captain, HMS Excellent, told to get on with the project at once".

Just five weeks later, on 8th October, Henry was appointed to the staff of *HMS Excellent*, serving as a Lieutenant RNVR in the School's Anti-Aircraft Department for the development and construction of a prototype Dome Teacher. In addition to Henry, a project team was assembled, including some of the staff of *Excellent*, Mr Oliver and Mr Gunn of Technicolor and representatives of Kodak. It was a landmark moment, and it was down to work right away. Henry's moment had come.

A difficulty emerged early on. Moving a cumbersome film projector through the necessary 'panning track' to match the original movements of the cine camera taking the aircraft attack films proved impossible. Inspired thinking on the part of Mr Gunn was to have the projector fixed, pointing towards the rear of the dome and project the film images onto a mirror reflecting the images onto the curved screen at the front dome wall. The mirror was mounted on a 'gimbal swivel' and movement controlled so that the image of the aircraft accurately followed the required panning track. The correct movements were achieved using a mechanical system comprising cams, rollers, wires and pulleys, driven by the film projector motor, such that the mirror movements were synchronised with the film.

To progress matters further, Henry then built a dome model to conduct experiments with reflected projections and determine the optimum position of the projector with respect to the mirror. In addition, he suggested a wood frame and plaster segment type construction for a full-scale prototype dome, incorporating blue internal lighting to give the impression of distance. A basic specification for the prototype was agreed during a meeting between Navy representatives and Technicolor, on 15th November. A half-dome of 25-foot radius was first constructed within the Old Racquets Court building at Whale Island. Step by step, the main components of Henry's idea were taking shape.

By now, Henry was looking into yet another technical challenge – the best means of pinpointing the ideal 'aiming-off' point (the point in front of the aircraft at which the trainee gunner needed to aim to score hits on a moving target). On top of that, the point, or Future Position Spot (FPS), had to be visible to the dome instructor but not the trainee, who needed to judge the amount of aim-off required. The FPS was a yellow dot superimposed onto relevant frames of the attack films. The team decided on fitting a yellow filter over the gunsight so the trainee wouldn't see the FPS.

A crucial milestone moment occurred in March 1941. The Inspector of Merchant Navy Gunnery, Sir Frederick C. Dreyer, was shown a mock up demonstration of the principal elements of the Dome Teacher. Sufficiently impressed, Dreyer actioned an order for 14 domes, even though the prototype was not yet complete. It provided the critical endorsement the project needed to press forward.

Technicolor were now engaged to manage the building of the dome prototype, adding to their existing responsibilities for aircraft attack film production and overseeing design and manufacture of dome equipment. With the project team at *Excellent* having laid down the detailed requirements, the Admiralty issued Technicolor with a contract order, dated 25th March 1941. This covered the construction and equipping of the 25-foot radius prototype Dome Teacher to be built at Whale Island, with a request "that you will now put the necessary work in hand as early as possible". The order also included supply of 14 specific attack films plus 2 non-specific, details of projection equipment, including the FPS, necessary soundtracks and associated items, range indicator details, and the need for suitable lighting and ventilation. The requirement for secrecy on the contract was made abundantly clear. The dome build was underway.

Elsewhere, other elements of the Dome A-A Trainer industry

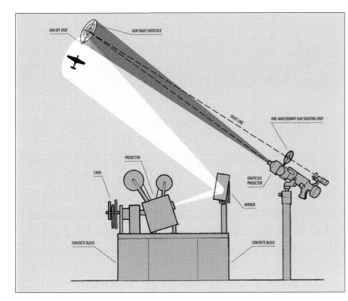

Above: The basic layout of the equipment used in the Dome Trainer.

were coming together – basic training for Dome Instructors and Technicians, compiling and printing of Operating Manuals and finally different sighting guns, from single Browning and Lewis type units to 40mm Bofors rigs. By mid-August, the Dome Teacher prototype was finished and details for production models determined and documented.

The Dome Trainer, as it became known, proved successful across all the services. There was some variation in materials used and internal equipment specification. Some domes, particularly smaller 20-foot diameter versions, were, for example, built of wood. Eventually, forty-six 40-foot diameter concrete and steel 'Technicolor type' domes were built for the RAF during the war at locations throughout Britain, with a further 66 'solid structure' domes supplied to them worldwide. The Army established domes at several UK locations, including London's Hyde Park. The overall number supplied to them by 1945 (UK and worldwide) reached 119. A total of 176 domes were supplied for the Navy for UK and worldwide use. These included 88 inflatable Portobel domes, a type developed and patented by Lieutenant Charles Bell, (the same Charles Bell who we heard earlier had worked to improve 'aim-off training'), after he saw the original prototype dome at Whale Island and began looking into possibilities for speeding up the construction process and refining the projection equipment.

By early 1944, Henry's pursuit of the Dome Teacher had spanned some four years. He worked tirelessly throughout, meeting various problems and challenges under conditions of considerable pressure and stress. This eventually took its toll. In the spring of 1944, Henry suffered a breakdown. He was placed on light duties whilst recuperating at home in London. Nevertheless, he continued to work, the Army granting him access to the dome in London's Hyde Park to "try out various small modifications".

Thankfully, Henry recovered his health and remained in Navy service for the rest of the war. He designed several other pieces of dome apparatus, including a new system for independent projection of the future position spot (increased aircraft speeds meant that the FPS could no longer be accommodated on the same film frame as the aircraft image). He also developed a 'hit recorder' instrument for registering successful shooting and a 'cloud/sky' background projection system to enhance realism.

The Dome Trainer had certainly come well and truly to life, shortening the odds in Britain's favour, but not without considerable personal cost to its determined inventor.

4. Langham's Dome

In early 1942 the Air Ministry turned its attention to UK dome locations. Already flying target tugs to service the local anti-aircraft training camps at Weybourne and Stiffkey, and about to undergo a massive redevelopment of the entire base, RAF Langham was an ideal site for a Dome Trainer.

By January 1942, the Air Ministry had endorsed a dome design developed by the Trussed Concrete Steel Co. Ltd., a London based subsidiary of a well-established American company. The official designation became Air Ministry Drawing 73/42.

Sometime in the first half of 1942 or possibly in 1943[2], Taylor Woodrow, the civil engineering company engaged as main contractor for Langham's upgrade, began the groundworks at the Dome site, adjacent to the Langham-Cockthorpe road running to the south of the airfield. Mains electricity was connected to the site prior to casting of the concrete footings and floor slab. Next in line was the Dome's frame, with vehicles arriving on site to deliver the prefabricated 'Truscon' dome steelwork set from the South Kensington factories of Trussed Concrete Steel Co. This included 16 main radial lattice box girders, a 5–foot diameter crown ring, numerous formed lattice box girder sections for the eight horizontal strengthening rings, intermediate reinforcing bars, additional frame-type reinforcing steel and large quantities of Hy-Rib steel mesh lathing strips.

A team of steel erectors now got to work as the main box girders were lifted into place, bolting the ring sections together with other reinforcing steels welded or bolted in as required. This new structure stood amongst the landscape awaiting its mantle. The build sequence continued with the fixing of Hy-Rib lathing over the entire internal surface, and the lower region of the external surface of the skeletal frame, to enable placing of concrete. As the truck mixers obliged, in a

Right: Air Ministry Drawing 73/42.

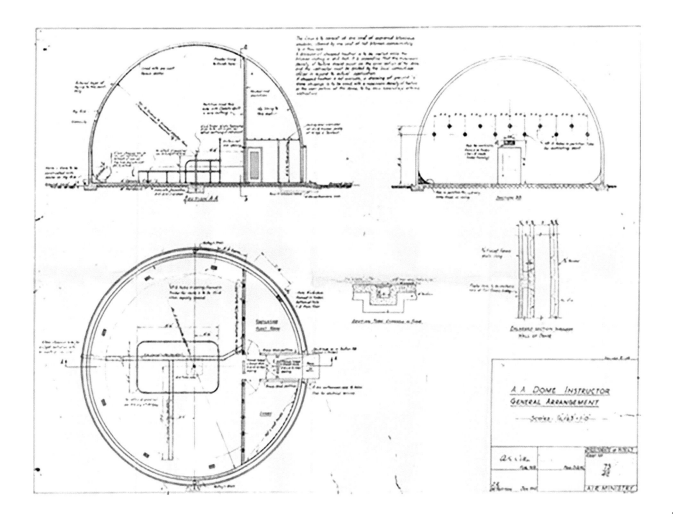

A A DOME INSTRUCTOR
GENERAL ARRANGEMENT

AIR MINISTRY

matter of days the dome had its solid walls. The newly placed walls were allowed to cure and strengthen before an external cement render and eventually, a bituminous waterproofing coat were added.

Internal work got underway within the Dome. A main quilt-lined partition wall was erected, separating off a quarter of the internal space. This was, in turn, sub-divided into a plant room for the required ventilation equipment and a further general-purpose room. Electrical wiring was completed, lighting fitted, soundtrack speakers and all items of technical equipment installed before guard rails were bolted into place. The main dome interior was covered with pre-formed plaster boards allowing application of a smooth plaster surface finish.

After fine tuning and commissioning, Langham's impressively named 'Apparatus Dome, A-A Training, No.1, Mk1' stood ready to do its work. Soon it echoed to the sound of aircraft, gunfire, falling bombs and the voices of instructors and would-be gunners alike, as the training programmes got well and truly underway.

5. Training in the Dome

As we've seen prior to Henry's invention, existing methods of anti-aircraft gunnery training were either rudimentary (to say the least) or involved use of real weaponry and live ammunition (both precious commodities) together with target tug aircraft. This was not only slow and enormously costly, but it could only train relatively small numbers of recruits. It also had many other limiting factors – bad weather or enemy action would limit training time, firing at towed drogue targets lacked the realism of air attack as they couldn't replicate the speed, manoeuvrability, variety and tactics of enemy aircraft in real air attacks. Offering an holistic solution, the Dome Trainer eliminated these limitations at a single stroke. Langham's doors were open for business.

The A-A gunnery recruits progressing on to Langham were mostly from the Army and RAF Regiment (the unit charged with airfield defence). Initially based at the Light A-A gunnery training camp at nearby Stiffkey, trainees completed the first part of their course involving classroom lectures and instruction on the features, characteristics and operation of specific weapon types, fire discipline and tactical control, together with subjects such as aircraft recognition, performance and role. They would have also been introduced to key A-A gunnery principles, particularly the technique of 'aiming-off' – that is, how far ahead of the target to allow, at the moment the gun is fired, the time taken for the bullet or shell to reach the required point so that it hits the aircraft. Not only that but, as the target was constantly moving, it followed that the 'aim-off' point must track the target's flight path. For recruits displaying a reasonable level of elementary knowledge and practical performance, it was on to Langham Dome.

After recruits had had a general introduction, the instructor would start sessions by turning on the blue background lighting, allowing a brief period for the trainee's eyes to adjust to the conditions. With one of the trainees in place at the 'dummy' gun, the instructor signalled the projectionist to run the first attack film. With new beginners, this would be one of the simpler, level-flying, single aircraft simulations. For the first few training sessions, the instructor would announce details of the aircraft type and speed, whilst the trainees concentrated on acquiring and tracking the target. At first, gunners were allowed to see the yellow future position spot (FPS) to get used to the direction and amount of aim-off required. After a few simulations, they either wore yellow glasses, or a yellow filter was added to the gunsight to render the FPS invisible to the trainee but crucially not the instructor. Obviously, it was important for the gunners not to see the yellow dot as in action they would need to judge the appropriate aim-off point for themselves in real time.

Trainees were taught not only where to fire but also when. The instructor would check the range indicator and, once the target was in range, tell the trainees when to open fire. As well as teaching the gunners to avoid wasting ammunition, it also enabled recruits to build up experience of judging viable range, again something they would need to do in a real air attack.

Using the position of the projected gun sight graticule in relation to the FPS yellow dot to monitor trainees' performance, the instructor focused initially on key subjects (directional aim and aim-off), pointing out errors as they were made, and offering advice on how the trainee could make corrections. Recruits awaiting their turn on the sighting units would observe the simulations from behind the guardrail and, very much part of the training, be asked for their observations and critical comments at the conclusion of each attack scenario.

When attack films were played, the dome's projector amplifier and loudspeaker system delivered aircraft engine noise, gunfire from the attacking aircraft, sounds of bombs being dropped and exploding, creating deafening effects enhanced by the dome's acoustics. Added to this was the noise of the trainee's own machine gun fire, produced by a dedicated gun-sound system when the gun trigger was pulled. These sound effects were an essential part of the training, acclimatising trainees to the noises they were to experience in action, making them less prone to panic or distraction during an attack. It's clear to see that every aspect of the training was considered and introduced specifically to maximise the chances of scoring hits on the enemy aircraft. This was virtual reality 1940s style – about 50 years ahead of its time.

As the recruits gained experience, the faster, more difficult attack simulations were introduced, including multi-aircraft scenarios. Trainees now experienced the short window available for an A-A gunner to aim and fire at a fast-attacking aircraft once in range – this was roughly only around 30 seconds! So, the importance of executing target pick up, range finding, aim-off and tracking as a smooth, instinctive sequence was abundantly clear. The instructor would then increase the difficulty level further by varying the routine and omitting details of the aircraft type and speed at the start of simulations. The training sessions were often quite lively, most recruits were generally enthusiastic and eager to get behind the sighting units at every opportunity. It was usually more of a question of how to get them out of the Dome rather than the reverse!

By this time, it would be apparent which trainees had the aptitude for the basic A-A gunnery techniques. Personnel failing to demonstrate the required level of competency were re-assigned to other duties. Having proved their overall competency, recruits that trained as single Light A-A gunners now progressed into service. For those on bigger gun batteries there was more.

As a 40-foot diameter dome facility, Langham accommodated training for not only single light A-A machine guns (Lewis, Browning or similar) but also the larger 40mm Bofors A-A guns. For successful completion of A-A gun instruction, all trainees had to demonstrate competency with the one-man Light Anti-Aircraft gun sighting unit. This also applied to 40mm A-A gun layers, (those in a gun crew concerned with moving and aiming the barrel of the larger guns); in order for them to continue training as part of a gun detachment, gun layers that passed the one-man sighting unit now trained as part of a team. The detachment consisted typically, of a gun commander, two gun layers (one operating the vertical movement and the other the horizontal), a Correctional Sight operator and a range setter. The Correctional Sight accounted for the speed of the target.

For this type of training, a 40mm gun platform replaced the one-man single gun unit. The 40mm platform consisted of a steel deck fitted with basic seating, gearing and hand operated wheels (the same as those used by the crew on an actual 40mm A-A gun mounting) plus a Correctional Sight. The rig was wheeled into the Dome and bolted in place behind the main mirror mounting.

As with the one-man gun unit, the training was progressive following a similar basic format and philosophy. In the early stages, the instructor selected the simpler attack films, provided advice and guidance on specific points and announced the aircraft type and speed. The gun commander gave the orders:

"aircraft approaching right", "engage target" and so on. At first, the gun layers received most of the training, practising initial target pick up, vertical and horizontal gun laying movements to achieve a smooth overall action. The instructor would assist with this, showing how the layers should move their hand wheels to ensure steady gun laying movements. As the range setter performed his task, the instructor checked his range settings were accurate and intervened if not.

Another part of the Correctional Sight mechanism was the Stiffkey Stick whose operator stood on a centrally located platform at the rear of the Bofors rig. The stick was a control for applying aim-off for the speed and direction of the target aircraft. When used, it automatically offset the two gun layers' sights by the right amount so initially, they only had to keep the centre of their respective sights on the target. The Stiffkey Stick operator was involved at this stage of the training but did not apply any aim-off. Instead, he practiced tracking the fuselage of the target aircraft.

Gradually, the gun layers became more proficient in engaging and tracking the target until the instructor could see, by the cross of light projected by the sighting unit, that their point of aim was maintained continuously on the aircraft. With more practice, the training moved on to cover fast target pick up and changing from one target to another for both gun layers and range setter. By now the gun drills should be smooth, instinctive sequences.

At this point, the Stiffkey Stick operator trained on loading the correct aim-off speed to the Correctional Sight. The gun layers then adapted the correct offset to the movement of their sights when the Stick operator applied the adjustment. The detachment should now be working truly as a team, the Stick operator building his experience over several training sessions, including judging the right moment to order "fire".

Finally, those trainee detachments that showed the necessary level of competency in the Dome, moved on to man the various A-A Batteries and Units of Britain's air defence.

Langham's Dome and others like it throughout the UK, together with the various types and numbers established world-wide, met the desperate need for efficient, effective anti-aircraft gunnery training. Henry Christian Stephens had delivered a solution at the critical moment. Britain had another valuable asset in its A-A defence and another step on the hard road to victory.

6. Closure and Renovation

Having been abandoned by the War Office, the airfield and all its infrastructures was eventually sold to Bernard Matthews plc, the well-known purveyor of turkey meat, in 1961. All those buildings that could be dismantled and removed, like hangars and Nissen huts, were auctioned off. Being a solid concrete structure, the Dome was not so easy to demolish so it was abandoned to the snoopers as well as the elements.

That is until the early 1980s. A former Battle of Britain pilot, Air Commodore Bertie Wootten, was driving across the airfield one day, with his wife, Ann, who happened to be the area District Councillor. As they passed the Dome he turned to her and said: "It's a shame that building is in such a state. It's so important to our history that it should be saved". Ann took the matter up at the Council and eventually English Heritage agreed that it was historically an important structure, so designated it as an 'Ancient Monument'. Bearing in mind it was only 40 or so years old, it was Norfolk's youngest ancient monument, if not the country's!

Patrick Allen, the Chairman of the Friends of Langham Dome, takes up the story:

"Over the next 10 years, there was considerable discussion between Martin Freeth, on behalf of the Langham Parish Council, English Heritage and Bernard Matthews plc. Bernard Matthews initially offered to undertake the preservation work at their own cost. However, in 1993 after six years of detailed consultation with English Heritage, Bernard Matthews decided to abandon those plans, partly due to the frustration of applying for scheduled monument consent, but also the soaring costs involved. My mother, Blanche Allen, Chair of the Parish Council, along with Langham resident, Ken Bartlett, spent many hours researching the airfield, advertising in RAF magazines and responding to letters from ex-servicemen who had been stationed at Langham.

"In early 1997, I had become Chairman of the Langham Parish Council, and the subject of the Dome was a regular item on the Parish Council meeting agendas. With a new millennium approaching, much talk of a Millenium Dome being built in London and the possibility of its acquiring money via the newly introduced National Lottery, the Council felt it was worth having another go at raising awareness of the existence of the village's very own Dome and its need for preservation – a worthy New Millennium project.

"At a meeting in May 1997 between myself and a Director of Bernard Matthews plc, whilst standing outside the Dome scratching our heads, a car pulled up and the occupant, a well-known Norwich architect, Sir Bernard Feilden, who lived in Stiffkey, approached us and enquired as to what was happening to the Dome. There was a further discussion about the lack of money needed for such a preservation project, to which Sir Bernard said he thought he might be able to help on that front. He suggested that there was an organisation called North Norfolk Historic Buildings Trust, led by a team of worthy Trustees and a chartered surveyor Malcolm Crowder. Subsequently a meeting was organised between Sir Bernard, Malcolm Crowder and myself, the result of which was that North Norfolk Historic

The Dome when surveyors reviewed its condition.

Buildings Trust would take on the project, working with the Parish Council, and English Heritage, to try and raise the funds need through the Heritage Lottery Fund and other grant providers."

During this period, North Norfolk Historic Buildings Trust (NNHBT) instigated a thorough feasibility study by a firm of structural engineers specialising in conservation, to assess what work was going to be needed in order to preserve the building for another 50 years. They produced a Conservation Plan along with a Performance Specification setting out the exacting operations required from specialist contractors in the repair and conservation of the concrete structure and its reinforcement.

In 2004, the Dome fronted press publicity for the launch of the English Heritage Buildings at Risk Register for the East of England. In response, English Heritage awarded a grant of £78,000 to further the work of feasibility and preservation. Now things were beginning to move. In September 2008, NNHBT purchased the Dome building, along with half an acre, from Bernard Matthews plc for the princely sum of £1!

Patrick picks it up again:

"We put together a formal application for a Stage 1 grant to the Heritage Lottery Fund. In October 2009 we were informed that this had been turned down. The main area of concern raised was the relatively isolated position of the Dome. Also concern about the strength of the community support and involvement to ensure the long-term sustainability of the project. However, the word from the grant officers was that we should not despair but tweak a few things, particularly their concern over community support, and then re-apply."

In January 2010 at a meeting in the Langham Village Hall the nucleus of a Friends of Langham Dome (FoLD) committee was formed. A constitution was drawn up and it was decided to ask for members to join at a one-off fee of £5. Following an 'open day' on the 26th June 2010, membership had gained momentum and reached over 140.

With this strong support a new application was submitted to the Heritage Lottery Fund for Stage 1 funding. This was successful and a grant of £18,100 was awarded. This enabled to NNHBT to press on with formulating a full bid to the Heritage Lottery Fund along with seeking out possible further funding from other organisations. It also enabled FoLD to develop as an organisation with the creation of a website and installing an information board outside the Dome. With everything in place, the application was finally submitted on the 28th November 2012.

Patrick concludes the saga:

"In March 2013 we heard that our application had been successful. An award of £446,000 had been made. On top of that £199,000 had been received from English Heritage; £15,000 from North Norfolk Historic Buildings Trust; £10,000 from Coastal Sustainability Fund; £5,000 from Norfolk County Council; £5,000 from North Norfolk District Council; £6,700 from Architectural Heritage Fund; Paul Bassham Trust £5,000; £10,000 from Pilgrim Trust; £5,000 from Community Landfill Trust."

With the funding now in place, work began in the Autumn of 2013 on the restoration of the building.

Right above: Restoration begins on the Dome.
Right below: The newly restored Dome in 2014.

On the fine summer's day of 19th July 2014, in a grand ceremony, the Dome was opened to visitors. To mark the occasion, the 'Grace' Spitfire carried out a wonderful display.

7. Legacy

After the war in 1946, the government set up a Royal Commission on Awards to Inventors to recognise and reward those individuals, whether members of the public or services, who made a significant contribution to the war effort. Henry had previously sought permission from the Admiralty to apply for a patent for his Dome invention but, to date, this had not been forthcoming. So, he submitted a claim to the Royal Commission.

Pursuit of a claim was, however, a substantial undertaking, not to be underestimated. Beyond preparation and submission of the basic claim, unless the matter was straightforward and could be settled by review and assessment of written evidence alone, submissions were conducted in the manner of a public courtroom trial. Evidence was presented by lawyers acting for the Crown and claimant, witnesses called to testify in person, and elements of cross examination by Crown counsel. Henry's was just such a case.

Henry engaged Messrs. Kilburn & Strode (Patent Agents) of Holborn, London. After the necessary preparatory work, an initial written claim was sent to the Secretary of the Commission, with a copy to the Admiralty, at the end of February 1947, arriving in the early days of March. Henry's claim covered right of invention for the unpatented Dome Trainer, Future Position Spot (patented), Hit Recorder (patented), Photographic Table and Background Scenic Effects for the Dome. Several witnesses were approached in support of his claim, these included, amongst others, Admiral Sir Frederick Dreyer GBE, KCB, CB, his brother- in-law, Commander Pigou, and his old friend Lt. Commander Guy Phelips.

The Admiralty replied to the Commission in early October 1947 stating that *"The Department admits that the Claimant had conceived the basic principle of the Dome Trainer prior to the date of his commission in the RNVR, but will contend that after such date he was assisted in the development and perfection of the Dome by officers of HMS Excellent and the staff of Technicolor Ltd."*

Henry's element of the hearing spanned four days from 5th to 8th of April, but with two counterclaims being submitted, it meant that the court proceedings continued until late April. Inevitably the stress and effort on Henry had taken its toll, imposing a great strain on his health so much so that by this time, he sustained a heart attack.

Henry did manage to pull through and the Commission's final decision, that had been delayed until the 28th May 1948, was eventually notified by letter to him from the Secretary of the Admiralty, Bath. The Commission's recommendation was that he receive an immediate payment of £1,000, "pending the final assessment of their award". A month later the Commission confirmed their decision and Henry was recognised as the inventor of the Dome Trainer. He had been awarded a total *ex gratia* payment of £5,000. Now Henry could take his much-needed rest.

Alas, he did not enjoy his reward for long. After just five short years, Henry died on the 5th June, 1953.

The Commission may have set a financial figure for Henry's invention, but it is impossible to calculate the contribution of the Dome Trainer – certainly in terms of potential lives saved. Today, looking back, we still can't draw a direct line between anti-aircraft defence and attacks that were thwarted, bombs that weren't dropped. Nor is it the case that Goering, because of the losses his Luftwaffe sustained from A-A gunfire, was inclined to halt the progress of the Blitz and thereby change the course of the war.

What we can say with confidence is that were it not for the determination and abilities of teams that worked the batteries on land and sea alike, so many of whom developed their skills in Dome Trainers, the devastation and losses incurred by air attack would have been far worse. We can say this because of a simple piece of logic. If there were no A-A guns fired at the enemy raiders, the attacking pilots and bomb aimers would have unhindered opportunity to ensure their payloads were delivered with the greatest of time and care. Any sane pilot under fire is not going to take that amount of time and care, plus the more accurate the defensive fire, the less time and care they'll take in favour of their own survival.

On a more practical note, the Dome Trainers saved thousands, if not millions, of pounds. We know that the percentage of trainees showing little or no aptitude for A-A gunnery skills was approximately 80%. Without Dome Trainers, the only way to determine whether a trainee had potential would have been to put every single trainee continually in front of a real gun, fully armed with real ammunition and somehow send up a real moving target to shoot at and, since this is training not real combat, without anyone getting killed or injured. The cost in terms of time, resource and money only to find out that 80% of the trainees had not been worth continuing with their training would have been astronomic. By selecting those who did show aptitude and more importantly by developing their skills further in the Dome Trainer, not only saved huge volumes of those scare resources, but significantly improved the ability of the gun crews in defending from air attack.

With the Dome Trainer, the right people were selected and their skills were honed, not just in the art of 'aiming-off', but also the myriad of other skills particular to ground-to-air defence, such as aircraft recognition, weapons management, range finding, etc.. All without firing a single round of ammunition.

'In 1942 we lost more than six and a half million tons of shipping by submarine attack, which nearly brought us to ruin. If on top of this, the air attacks had continued on the heavy scale of the early part of 1941, I am of the opinion that we should have been completely ruined... I had an office at Admiralty and got going at once to teach the Merchant Navy what I called 'Pheasant Shooting at Sea'. I realised at once that Stephens had in effect thrown us a lifebuoy in our time of greatest distress... The 'horror of the Blitz' attacks at sea had been dispelled by Stephens. The value of the shipping and cargoes saved by the improved standard of shooting resulting from the training which the Merchant Navy gunners, and the Navy and Army gunners on board the ships received in the Dome Trainer was immense.'

Admiral Sir Fredrick Dryer, GBE, KCB, Royal Navy Inspector of Merchant Navy Gunnery (1941–1945)

Add to this, the fact that Henry's technology still endures, as Domes remain a vital training resource for the armed forces today, demonstrates how far-sighted his ingenuity extends.

Right: Henry Christian Stephens – innovator and visionary.

Henry Stephens's legacy, then, is immeasurable. We are so used to the extraordinary simulations that computers now display with such life-like accuracy that it's easy to dismiss the comparatively rudimentary technology we see in our working restoration at Langham Dome. But let us not forget that Henry Stephens achieved a virtual simulation before microchips were even imagined never mind made possible. Furthermore, what his inventive, creative mind brought to bear during the darkest of times was not only technical originality but also surely a sense of hope and confidence that such ingenuity provided a decisive edge in standing against aggression.

Through documentaries and dramatizations, we are now familiar with, and indeed celebrate, the genius of someone such as Alan Turing and his work developing the concept of the modern computer. Surely Henry's invention and development of virtual reality, well before the age of microchips, was equally visionary and should equally be celebrated and disseminated.

Thankfully the Langham Dome Museum stands as such a testament to a unique talent.

Part II: RAF Langham

On VE Day 8th May 1945, the day Germany surrendered to the Allied Command, the Operations Log at RAF Langham makes no mention of the significance of the date. The station recorded a number of routine sorties, mainly patrols and some meteorological flights. The Log merely notes: "All patrols rendered negative reports". A quiet day by all accounts. A few months later on 2nd September, the Japanese surrendered. The war was over.

Six long years earlier almost to the day, British hearts collectively sank to the floor. It was 3rd September, 1939 at 11.15 a.m. when the Prime Minister, Neville Chamberlain, broadcast to the nation those unforgettable words, crackling across the airwaves:

"This morning the British Ambassador in Berlin handed the German Government a final Note stating that, unless we heard from them by 11 o'clock that they were prepared at once to withdraw their troops from Poland, a state of war would exist between us.

I have to tell you now that no such undertaking has been received, and that consequently this country is at war with Germany."

It had been only twenty years since the so-called Great War – the 'war to end all wars' as it was popularised by US President Woodrow Wilson – had eventually come to a close. It was still raw in the minds of those that huddled round their radios listening to Chamberlain. What would this new conflict bring to the nation? Trepidation and uncertainty spread across the land.

On the day after war was declared, the Royal Air Force received a message from His Majesty King George VI, who had himself served in the RAF toward the end of the First World War. It read:

"The Royal Air Force has behind it a tradition no less inspiring than those of the older Services… you will have to shoulder far greater responsibilities than those which your Service had to shoulder in the last war… I can assure all ranks of the Air Force of my supreme confidence in their skill and courage and their ability to meet whatever calls will be made upon them."

What follows is the true story of how that responsibility was actually "shouldered" by those who played their part at RAF Langham. It is by turns inspiring, tragic, heroic, astonishing, sometimes amusing but above all memorable. Of the men and women that served at RAF Langham, one hundred and twenty that answered those "calls made upon them" in the Second World War did not live to tell their tale.

Some of those tales are now told here.

1. Then and Now

Take any sunny day in North Norfolk, indeed across the whole county, and amongst the gently rolling meadows, you will not be too far away from an airfield. Most of them are now disused but it was a different story in the dark days of the Second World War. Whereas in the 1940s, on a similar day, the Norfolk skies would have been almost alive with the sight and sound of fighters or bombers heading off on one sortie or another. Today, the mellifluous songs of skylarks and the circling raucous rooks dominate the heavens.

The prevalent feature that now endures as testament to the existence of these once abundant sites is usually the remains of a runway. Other than our very own Dome, this is certainly the case at Langham. The road to Cockthorpe running outside the Dome is interrupted here and there with stretches of concrete, evidence of the runways and perimeter track that once comprised RAF Langham airfield. The keen observer will also spy amongst the trees to the north of the Dome another lasting legacy – a small collection of buildings that includes the old Control Tower. All the rest are gone – save for a few patches of foundation work on which they once stood.

That said, Langham was not necessarily a total stranger to the presence of aircraft. The photo on page 43 is of Benny Hucks, an early pioneering aviator, having landed just off Langham's Binham Road in a Blériot XI some time before the First World War, probably as early as 1913 only ten years after the first powered flight by the famous Wright brothers. The gentleman in the rear seat, clearly enjoying himself, is the grandfather of the current Chair of the Trustees of Langham Dome.

The tranquillity we now experience outside our diminutive museum belies the once febrile activity of the war years. Within shouting distance of Langham were five other RAF airfields, all buzzing with activity during the war: Bircham Newton, Docking, Little Snoring, North Creake and Sculthorpe.

Remarkably, prior to the outbreak of war in the September of 1939, the quietude was even more profound than today. The serenity we now recognise in North Norfolk is only a shadow of the sense of peace and quiet residents knew then. Agriculture dominated the landscape and the lives of its residents. In 1939 there were just five operational airfields across the whole county – Bircham Newton, Feltwell, Marham, Watton and West Raynham. By the end of the war there were thirty-seven.

2. Norfolk and Langham Between the Wars

Norfolk, in common with all British rural counties, did not emerge from the war of 1914-18 untouched. You need only

Farm workers in 1930s North Norfolk take a break.

to pass through any village in the county to see a memorial to those local men and boys (some were that young) who did not come home. Langham has one. Not so evident as many perhaps but there, nonetheless.

After the 'war to end all wars', life outside the main towns in Norfolk returned to its familiar round of agricultural activities. Affairs of state were, for most local people, of little or no consequence – part of a completely different world to that of the plough and scythe. The north of the county especially was sparsely populated. Mobility and communication were not only extremely limited but scarcely featured. Most locals,

if they did go on holiday, only made it as far as Sheringham or Cromer. Few people came to Norfolk and few people left. Being largely surrounded by sea to the north and east, Norfolk was, literally, on the road to nowhere.

Not surprising, then, that news of world events such as the foreboding Spanish Civil War[3] in the late 1930s failed to register any particular importance for the folk of rural North Norfolk. More pressing rather, local talk concentrated on the cultivation and husbandry consequences of the bitterly cold

Right: Benny Hucks (standing) in his Blériot XI .

weather encountered as 1938 turned the corner into what would become the profoundly dark year of 1939.

Unlike much of the rest of the world, having left the scars of 1914-18 behind, few in North Norfolk sensed the air of conflict brewing on the horizon. Yet Europe was a powder keg. Increased nationalistic and extreme right-wing ideologies were taking hold especially in Spain, Italy and Germany. Similar tensions emerged in the Orient. The expansionist movement in Japan in the 1930s fuelled by increased militarism seriously destabilised the Far East. All through the 1930s, those right-wing nationalistic movements not only seized political power in their countries, but, once in government, the expansionist ambitions of their leaders soon turned to the invasion of their neighbours.

In Langham though, the world turned slowly. The early days of 1939 in this sleepy little hamlet and its surrounding countryside would offer the occasional visitor a picture of apparent idyllic rural timelessness as though it had been untouched in centuries. Compared with today, it might seem almost feudal. A farm worker earned around £1/15s a week (£1.75 in today's money) and would likely as not be employed by the local landed gentry. Given a house in the area may cost perhaps £500, on those wages most families could not afford their own property and consequently rented and lived in 'tied' cottages owned by their wealthy employer. School leaving

The war memorial in Langham village.

age was fourteen and children followed in the footsteps of their parents, married other local youngsters and settled into the same life as previous locals going back many generations.

Needless to say, then, when war did inevitably break out, the 300 or so population of Langham were not in the least prepared for the arrival of the Royal Air Force right in their back yard.

3. The Early Years: 1940-41

During 1939, the Air Ministry requisitioned land, often farmland, across the whole eastern side of Britain. Being the furthest east and therefore closer to the Continent, land in Norfolk was a particular target and the patch of land between Cockthorpe and Langham was an ideal site. Originally with grass runways, the airfield was built during the first few months of the Second World War as a dispersal and satellite station[4] to RAF Bircham Newton.

The idea of satellite airfields was to extend the facilities of the parent station, and, where necessary, serve as a substitute. In addition to training and emergency, satellites could be used by RAF maintenance units to disperse aircraft from parent stations to minimise the risk of damage or loss due to enemy air attacks. Some basic maintenance and upgrades could also be carried out at these fields.

Docking[5] and Langham were selected as satellite airfields for RAF Bircham Newton. In due time, both satellites would go on to become independent stations but, until that point, Bircham remained in overall control.

Already an established main RAF station[6], Bircham Newton had opened originally in 1916 but remained largely inactive during the First World War. It was re-opened in the 1920s as a bomber station until, under the 1936 restructuring of the RAF[7], the station was assigned to 16 Group Coastal Command. It saw significant development over the years and its grass runways once again saw use by a variety of single- and twin-engined aircraft. The station became a cornerstone of Coastal Command during World War II and handled several vital operational roles.

Meanwhile, in its support role, Langham became operational in the summer of 1940. The first activities at the airfield were less than exciting. In order to support the anti-aircraft firing ranges at nearby Stiffkey and Weybourne, target tug aircraft were stationed at Bircham. The aircraft of 'K' and 'M' Flights No. 1 AACU (Anti-Aircraft Co-Operation Unit) were refuelled at Langham on a daily basis. Initially only a skeleton squad of around twenty fliers, a fire crew and support personnel were deployed there from Bircham.

At first, some local inhabitants took exception to the presence of an airfield on the surrounding farmland. This discontent presented itself rather unusually with instances of stone-throwing at aircraft parked close to the Cockthorpe road! The resultant damage was not extensive, but nevertheless sufficient to prompt a hasty revision of aircraft parking locations.

That wasn't all the ground crews had to contend with though. On an airfield devoid of buildings, flimsy canvas covered metal-framed engine tents, pitched over the noses

The Morston Road, Langham with villagers and servicemen walking in the quiet of the day.

of the aircraft, were the only shield against the elements for aircraft and ground crews alike. The bone-chilling nature of North Norfolk winters was something etched forever in the minds of many who served at Langham on those days.

Other than this, life took on a relatively quiet routine for those first few RAF personnel at Langham. Many of them were billeted at Langham Hall, a large imposing Georgian building that was originally the rather grand residence of the local vicar in the 1820s. The Blue Bell pub proved a welcome source of diversion to the servicemen. Other than that, and the occasional trip to the cinema at nearby Holt, it was a fairly subdued beginning for RAF Langham. But that was never going to last.

New Year's Day 1941 brought the first tragedy to RAF Langham. A Lockheed Hudson of 206 Squadron based at Bircham was on a routine flight to Langham to give two new pilots local familiarisation. It is believed the pilot may have been demonstrating dive bombing techniques when the aircraft hit a barn with its wing tip while flying low and crashed. Everyone on board – eight in total – was killed including three unfortunate ground crew who had only joined the flight by hitching what they thought was an easy ride to Langham.

Over the next year, a variety of aircraft types flew in and out of Langham. Bristol Blenheim MkI/IVs from Bircham were dispersed here on a number of occasions during 1941. The grass field continued to be used by Hudsons from Bircham, especially for departing or returning from operations at night, the very primitive lighting at Langham being better than none at Bircham. Similarly, Vickers Wellingtons of 221 Squadron flew their night maritime patrols and night training exercises from Langham in 1940 and 1941. In addition, Wellingtons of Bomber Command used Langham to practice emergency landings during training flights carried out in 1941 and 1942.

It wasn't all 'back room' support work, however. Langham was occasionally involved in operational attack sorties. The most notable from this early period occurred on the night of the 23rd/24th March 1941. In conjunction with several other squadrons, 300 Squadron, made up of Polish airmen, received orders to prepare for participation in a raid on Berlin. Based at RAF Swinderby, Lincolnshire, under the control of No.1 Group, at the time 300 Squadron were operating the twin-engined Wellington Mk IC medium bomber. On this occasion, the squadron was authorised to use the more easterly RAF satellite airfield at Langham as an advanced operating base, thereby reducing the range to target. Seven 300 squadron crews were selected for the operation under the leadership of Wing Commander Makowski.

During Sunday 23rd March, the crews were briefed, and the seven Wellingtons flew over to Langham, where their fuel tanks were topped up in readiness for the night ahead. Each aircraft carried maximum loads that included several 500lb bombs and cannisters of incendiaries. Squadron take-off time was set for 22.00 hrs.

As the day progressed however, weather conditions deteriorated – wind, rain and steadily worsening visibility increased until the point where the operation was threatened. Despite this, Wg Cdr Makowski led the squadron off on time, his departure being logged at 22.04 hrs. Three more Wellingtons were airborne within the next twenty minutes.

So far so good, four aircraft up and underway. Next across Langham's grass was aircraft code sign 'BH-M', piloted by Sgt. Kazmierczak. All seemed well at first, but then disaster struck. As his Wellington struggled to get airborne, it experienced

Left to right: Pilots Makowski, Cwynar and Dziekonski (photo from later in the war).

a violent swing, causing the aircraft to plough through the boundary fence and crash into adjacent fields. Incredibly, all six crew walked away unharmed.

Having seen what happened to his compatriot and under mounting tension, Squadron Leader Cwynar brought his 'BH-R' to the threshold and commenced his run. Alarmingly, his aircraft suffered a similar fate to its predecessor. A vicious swing on take-off pushed the Wellington off the runway and through the perimeter fence to crash in the fields beyond.

Once again, all six crew members survived unhurt.

At this point, enough might well have been enough, but these were Polish airmen in exile from their occupied homeland with a chance to strike directly at the Nazi capital. Motivation was high. The seventh and last Wellington lined up. Unfortunately, after more than one effort to get in the air, the bomber sustained some damage and was forced to abandon any further attempts.

Meanwhile, oblivious to the events unfolding behind, the four airborne Wellingtons continued to their distant target. Sgt. Hajdukiewicz, arriving too early, overshot Berlin. Instead, he delivered his bombs on buildings located some 15 miles to the south-east of the target, then made a safe return to Langham. Next to arrive, Flight Lieutenant Sulinski had better luck. He reached Berlin at 01.40 hrs where his bomb aimer successfully dropped their bombs over the course of two runs. He then dropped leaflets near Magdeburg, before returning to land at RAF Sutton Bridge. In the third aircraft, Sgt. Dziekonski also reached Berlin and released his bombs. He noted three corresponding bursts, judged to be approximately 1 mile south-west of the target. He ultimately landed at RAF Waddington.

The last of the four to arrive over what he thought was Berlin, Wg Cdr Makowski released one 500lb bomb. He then spotted a concentration of searchlights and flak some distance

Some of the Polish crew members of 300 Squadron at Swinderby just before heading off to Langham.

ahead. He immediately calculated that this must be part of Berlin's main defences and that his bomb was therefore short. Makowski pushed on, only to find that the concentration was in fact a decoy site. Venturing further, he finally dropped his remaining load of three bombs and two cannisters of incendiaries on buildings somewhere probably north-east of Hannover.

One raid, an initial piece, but a piece nonetheless, in a mosaic that would build and build as the war went on.[8] Part of a beginning, a means of fighting back. Langham had had its first taste of major frontline action.

By the end of 1941, the 'Phoney War' was well and truly over.

First, the heroic but nonetheless humbling evacuation of Dunkirk in May/June 1940 rocked the country. The latter end of 1940 saw the Luftwaffe throw everything at Britain. The war was suddenly and starkly no longer phoney but very real indeed. Many feared the country would be invaded, but the Battle of Britain amazingly staved off Operation Sealion – the German code name for the invasion of the United Kingdom. The Blitz of London and other major cities and industry followed. It continued relentlessly for the next eight months.

Now there was war on every front. Rommel[9], Germany's much acclaimed 'Desert Fox', landed his Afrika Korps in Tripoli, the campaign against German and Italian forces in North Africa began. Further afield, first Yugoslavia then Greece capitulated to German forces, all in the space of a month. German forces seemed unstoppable as they then stormed through large parts of Russia. The outlook was bleak.

In common with the rest of the country, no one in North Norfolk was now under any further illusion that the country was not at war. Rationing had been introduced in 1940. School children from London were evacuated to the eastern counties in early 1941 and later that year the largest ever exercise was undertaken to simulate an invasion of East Anglia. Alongside the military activity in the area, defence emplacements were cropping up everywhere. It was difficult to move between the inland towns and the North Norfolk coast without seeing an anti-aircraft gun battery. The Dome at Langham, though not yet built, would in time prove itself a vital resource in training those gun crews.

To support the war effort, Norfolk farmers had been set ploughing quotas, which they proudly exceeded, and, in one piece of good news, farm workers were awarded a new minimum wage of £3 a week. In order to supplement farm workers in feeding the nation, the government started the Women's Land Army in July 1939 under the control of the Ministry of Agriculture and Fisheries. Known as the Land Girls, most already lived in the countryside but more than a third came from London and the industrial cities of the north of England. All in all, there were 1,650 Land Girls in Norfolk during the war, many helping the farmers meet their quotas.

Locally, for the people of Langham and nearby Cockthorpe, war arrived in startling and terrifying fashion. There had been a couple of small sporadic raids on the newly-established airfield in the autumn of 1940 but nothing too severe. That all changed on February 11th, 1941. The base was attacked by the Luftwaffe with 100 incendiary bombs dropped in the area. Not only that, but the Germans had clearly taken note of the RAF activity at Langham and by 1941 the Luftwaffe had opened a file on Langham in their official Target Folder. Consequently, they launched a huge attack on 11th April – 500 incendiaries and 7 high-explosive bombs – followed by another attack on 17th with 60 high-explosives then two smaller attacks on 21st and 23rd .

Thankfully, at the end of 1941, things quietened down as the base was temporarily closed for building work. Unbeknown to the locals though, that was actually just a precursor to some profound changes afoot. If the residents of Langham were at last beginning to get used to the sight and sound of a wartime airfield on their doorstep, not to mention the occasional uniformed personnel wandering around the village, they were about to get a rude awakening as things were about to escalate at their military neighbour just down the road. Expanding its role in support of the nearby live firing ranges, on 6th December 1941 'K' and 'M' Flights of No. 1 AACU arrived from Bircham Newton bringing twelve Hawker Henleys, two de Haviland Tiger Moths, one Westland Lysander and about two hundred personnel!

That was not the end of the story. With the airfield being the most northerly of the wartime RAF airfields in Norfolk and its position just a few miles from the North Sea, it made an ideal site to be a fully-fledged independent operational base for RAF Coastal Command aircraft. The true purpose behind the recent building work and new arrivals had now become apparent. RAF Langham was about to take on a life of its own. So began the next important chapter in the life of the North Norfolk outpost.

Hawker Henley target tugs flew from Langham with No1 AACU.

4. Independence and Coastal Command: 1942

On 16th July 1942, the first entry, handwritten, in RAF Form 540 (a station's official Operations Record Book) reads:

Place	Date	Time	Summary of Events	SECRET.
LANGHAM	16.7.42.		RAF Station LANGHAM officially opened as an independent unit under the command of Group-Captain T.H. CARR AFC, DFC.	

"RAF Station LANGHAM officially opened as an independent unit under the command of Group-Captain T.H. CARR AFC, DFC."

The son of Major-General Howard Carr, C.B., Terence Carr was a regular officer in the Royal Air Force prior to the outbreak of the war. Before arriving at Langham, he had already shown determined leadership and bravery in carrying out several offensive operations including attacks on enemy ports, vessels and flak ships.

In 1940, after promotion to the rank of Wing Commander, he was given command of 220 Squadron. He led his Lockheed Hudson crews on patrols over the Dunkirk beaches as protection for the servicemen of the BEF while they boarded the rescue ships. In acknowledgement of his actions, he was awarded the Distinguished Flying Cross. But recognition of his accomplishments did not stop there. For his gritty and dogged efforts in the rescue of an aircrewman, adrift in a dinghy for 84 hours in appalling conditions, Carr was also awarded the Air Force Cross. His citation read:

"Wing Commander Carr maintained contact with the dinghy for five and a half hours, only giving up when darkness set in. The search was continued in vain on the next two days, but on the 27th September, during his second search that day, Wing Commander Carr found the dinghy and remained over it for four hours, until surface craft reached and rescued the sole survivor."

Having taken up the reins at Langham, there was no time for the new Station Commander, or any of the new personnel posted there, to take a breath and admire the view. The very day after that opening entry in the Operations Log, six aircraft arrived for operational duties. But oddly they were not from an RAF unit. They were in fact from 819 Squadron of the Fleet Air Arm on loan to Coastal Command and under the command of Lieutenant H. S. McN. Davenport, R.N.. They had flown down all the way from Machrihanish on the west coast of Scotland just north of the Mull of Kintyre.

The aircraft were somewhat unusual too. The Fairey Swordfish was a biplane and, even by the standards of the day, looked old-fashioned and unwieldy – none of the sleek lines of a Spitfire here. No, this ungainly bucket of bolts harked back to the airframe structure of First World War aircraft[10].

Right: The Fairey Swordfish or 'Stringbag'.

Affectionately nicknamed 'Stringbag' because of the wire braces between the upper and lower wings, the Swordfish was usually deployed on aircraft carriers in an anti-shipping torpedo attack role. Even more unusual, Navy Swordfish sported a white livery yet the six aircraft at Langham were ominously all black. They were in readiness for night operations minelaying in the North Sea to disrupt German naval activity.

At least the airfield was beginning to take shape as a proper RAF station, rather than a dispersal site, with a few modest buildings now dotted around the perimeter including a few Blister hangars on the north side of the strip for use in servicing the aircraft. Just as well, because by the end of the month, the personnel stationed at the base had increased even further to a little over 600.

And still the aircraft arrived in numbers. Commanded by Wing Commander A. E. Rogenhagen, 280 Squadron transferred from Bircham swelling the ranks with fourteen Avro Ansons, responsible for coastal patrol, reconnaissance and air-sea rescue along East Anglia and the south coast of England.

Over the next few months, the Ansons of 280 Squadron were out on air sea rescue search patrols over the North Sea almost every day. It was a largely thankless task as most of the time they either found nothing or sometimes an oil slick or pieces of debris. Only on a few occasions did they spot someone to rescue at which point the crew would radio in the position and drop a smoke float in order to 'fix' the survivor for a rescue vessel to pick them up. Sometimes they would sight a dinghy but too often, as they approached, dispiritingly found no signs of life.

On the 18th of August, 1942 the war came knocking on the door again as the Luftwaffe paid a most unwelcome visit. Around 300 incendiary bombs were dropped around Langham by German bombers. It's not clear what damage was sustained, and the Station's Operations Log makes no mention of it. Presumably there was little harm done to the runway as the Log on the day simply notes that six Ansons of 280 Squadron went out on an area search in the hopes of finding an aircraft believed to have ditched in the sea. The search was unsuccessful. However, the bombing raid reminded the local residents that, despite living in a small, rural village, danger in wartime 1940s Europe was never far from your door.

By contrast, life for the more seasoned personnel at Langham airfield had by now fallen into a fairly steady routine. Air sea rescue searches by the crews of 280 Squadron dominated the operations with target tug flights by 1AACU continuing in support of the local firing ranges. To everyone's relief there

Right: An Avro Anson on coastal patrol.

were few losses on any of these flights. The most notable piece of excitement came late in the year when Army Cooperation Command arrived for a brief stay to support army manoeuvres in North Norfolk with 2 Squadron Mustangs and 231 Squadron Tomahawks filling the runways.

Meanwhile over the course of 1942, the war abroad had taken on a very different and sombre aspect. Following the attack on Pearl Harbor in December 1941, America had entered the war. Whilst welcome in respect of a new and very powerful ally for the British campaigns, the consequences were that the war was now most assuredly global. Norfolk wasn't immune. Over several nights in late April and early May 1942, during what became known as the 'Baedeker raids',[11] German planes bombed Norwich, dropping over 90 tons of incendiary and high explosives that caused 67 deaths. The raids were so punishing, some in North Norfolk reported seeing the orange glow of Norwich burning to the south.

Neither was this escalation in the conflict about to pass the people of Langham by. The airfield was about to undergo a massive transformation with more planes and personnel than ever before. Yes, the locals had noticed a difference as operations had intensified when the station became fully independent but, important as they were, providing target tugging and air sea rescue duties was still a fair step away from the front line. That was about to change beyond anything the locals had seen so far. Plans were now laid for Langham to step up from its support role. It was about to become a major base for Coastal Command.

The closing entry in the Operations Record Book on 3rd November 1942 at 17:00hrs states succinctly:

"RAF Station Langham ceased to be an operational unit with effect from this date and was handed over to Care and Maintenance Unit."

These were the workers who were about to transform RAF Langham into a serious war machine.

5. Rebuilding: 1943

The construction workers arriving at Langham in late 1942 and early 1943 were part of the huge industry of airfield construction that had evolved over the preceding eight years and had now reached a point of peak production. Working to a proven set of designs, their task was to elevate Langham to 'Class A' airfield status and ensure that it re-joined the fray fully equipped and ready for its new front line role.

So, who were these construction teams, what plans governed the works to be undertaken and what exactly did the schedule of 'Class A' works entail?

The Airfield Construction Programme remains the largest construction project in the country's history. Leading civil engineering companies, including today's familiar names of John Laing & Sons, Taylor Woodrow, Wimpey and Robert McAlpine, were contracted for the works. In most cases, construction of the new airfields involved a combination of contractors working in conjunction to co-ordinated site plans and a schedule of works produced and overseen by the Air Ministry.

The construction of a typical airfield would entail:
- at least one runway of 2,000 yards
- aircraft hangers of 240ft x 115ft
- 10 miles of drains
- two underground fuel dumps of 100,000 gallons capacity each
- a sewage works

all at a cost very often exceeding £800,000 (£35m in 2023 according to the Bank of England).

And the 'tools for the job'? The requirement for heavy plant, everything from bulldozers and excavators to tipper lorries and concrete mixers, was supplied via Air Ministry allocations of existing British held equipment supplemented by Lend-Lease shipments from America.

A large workforce was called for. In the early days, an Irish contingent formed the core of this labour force that would swell to around 60,000 by 1942. The work was demanding to say the least. They worked in constant shifts, '24-7'. The pioneering nature of the design, construction techniques and the variety of materials used, was challenging too. There was much on-the-job learning over the years as the workforce gained valuable experience. Come the end of 1942, they passed through Langham's gates a highly organised, effective machine. By that time, this formidable force had already increased the number of operational RAF stations in Britain to 510 with a further 150 in prospect. Langham was next in line.

One key factor, established at the outset in the interests of both efficiency and economy of production, was the principle of using off-the-shelf standard designs. The designs covered every possible aspect of construction from the bare essentials (latrines, heating systems) to the crucially important (hangars and runways). This meant large numbers of airfields were built at relatively low cost and in a fairly short space of time – mass-produced almost, which proved crucial in Britain keeping pace with German rearmament. It is also why so many airfields of the time look very similar.

By 1942, the Class 'A' airfield design (derived from a 3-runway layout configured in an 'A' shape) had been adopted as the standard for bomber stations and the reference model for the construction of new airfields and updating existing ones. This was the design for Langham.

The main contractor for the upgrade was Taylor Woodrow. The challenge facing them amounted to the equivalent of building a small town and would require the corresponding infrastructure, power, mains water, drainage, sewers and sewage disposal works. Then the main Class 'A' elements: three intersecting concrete runways, taxiways, hard standings, a technical and administration site comprising a whole raft of buildings supporting the day-to-day operations of the station including the Headquarters, squadron offices and crew rooms.

On top of that there were all the facilities for the servicing, repair, maintenance and storage of aircraft, a second fuel installation, a bomb storage area, specialist buildings like the Battle HQ (which was an underground bunker), Dome A-A Teacher, Bombing Trainer and a host of smaller buildings and installations. In fact, over 140 structures of one sort or another plus further works at the dispersed sites beyond the airfield (eventually there would be 12 sites in all, including a sick quarters). Things around Langham were going to be anything but peaceful. The earth was quite literally going to move!

Borne out of experience on earlier sites, a major initial priority was the laying down of the perimeter track, a 50ft wide concrete pavement extending around the entire boundary of the main airfield. This had a dual purpose. Once the base was operational again, it allowed for aircraft movement and dispersal away from the main runways. For the construction period, however, it served perfectly as a haulage road covering the entire works site. With the site largely made up of unsurfaced ground, it proved a vital main artery allowing access to the area for the site vehicles, heavy plant and delivery lorries bringing in materials and equipment to feed this ever-hungry entity and the construction workers housed in its midst. The shuddering start-up and deep bass roar of powerful diesel engines rose-up as the machine operators, banksmen and groundworkers swung into gear.

Descendants of the so-called navvies (the 'navigators' who dug the canals and laid the roads and railways during the Victorian era), this project was meat and drink to the construction workers. The art of moving, shaping and preparing ground was their heritage. Employing familiar methods, if more mechanised, this was an altogether larger-scale version of digging for victory.

As sections of the perimeter track were completed, infrastructure works began at other locations; excavation for drains, cables and sewers, footings and foundations and preparation and placing of ground-bearing concrete slabs. On the perimeter track itself, groups of 'spectacle loop' type hard standings (see the aerial photo overleaf) for aircraft dispersal appeared gradually at intervals all around the airfield as the groundworkers hit their stride. Now other sub-contract trades came into play: scaffolders, steel erectors, bricklayers, carpenters, electricians, and plumbers swelled the ranks as the programme gained momentum.

Then there were the runways, major sub-projects in themselves demanding a considerable amount of preparation and huge amounts of material. As winter gave way to the spring and summer of 1943, the excavator, bulldozer, blade scraper and steam-roller drivers applied their skills, working long days to first clear, then level and grade massive strips of ground for the respective 2,000-yard main and 1,400-yard secondary runways, before compacting down thousands of tons of hardcore to form the necessary sub-bases.

Scarcity of suitable local rock types meant that an alternative source had to be found for this hardcore. Again, an innovative solution presented itself. Earlier in the airfield programme, they came up with the idea of transporting trainloads of rubble from London buildings destroyed in the Blitz. These were now steaming daily by train into East Anglia for onward distribution by road to the airfield construction sites. A fitting use, perhaps, for this unfortunate by-product, it was simply a matter of adding Langham's name to the destination list.

Next in the constant stream of materials came a mass of concrete, placed, and compacted to a thickness of some 6 to 9 inches over the 150ft width of each runway. Finally, after weeks of curing, the paving machines moved in to apply a surface finish of pitch-like asphalt. Langham's grass was changed forever.

By early Spring 1944, the workforce had begun to move out. True, some finishing work was yet to be completed, one main hangar was still a steel skeleton for example, but, crucially, Langham was ready to operate.

It was some feat, as they moved on to pastures new, the construction teams had delivered Langham's upgrade in just 16 months. The scene was now set, soon new occupants would arrive to take up the sword.

The year 1943 was when the momentum changed. The Axis Powers – Germany, Italy and Japan – were no longer on the front foot. Early that year, the North African campaign concluded with Rommel's forces in full retreat and the victorious General (later Field Marshall) 'Monty' Montgomery being hailed as a master tactician[12]. The Americans joining the war had made a profound difference. Japanese gains in the Pacific and the Far East were beginning to be retaken by Allied counter-invasion. US Airforce bombers arrived in East Anglia to take up daytime bombing raids against German targets whilst British aircraft were pounding Germany at night.

With this change in impetus, the tone of the war had changed in the mood of the people at home. The British Government now believed the threat of German invasion had passed. In December 1943 General Dwight D. Eisenhower was appointed Supreme Commander the Allied Expeditionary Force in Europe to spearhead the forthcoming invasion of continental Europe.

Operation Overlord, as it was known, was already in preparation. The Norfolk coast was now a huge training ground for beach landings. The whole county was awash with troops simulating attacks on all sorts of installations. Now, with no small sense of irony, the same structures that were originally placed there in anticipation of repelling a German invasion were providing the perfect scenarios to practice assaulting German emplacements.

The German war effort relied heavily on the supply of high-grade iron ore from occupied Norway and neutral Sweden.

Convoys, large and small, of merchant ships protected by heavily armed escort vessels were steaming along the coastlines of Norway and the Low Countries delivering these supplies to mainland Germany on a largely daily basis. Now the tide had changed in favour of the Allies, it was vital to stop this flow of material and tighten the grip on German industry.

Langham was about to go on the offensive.

Right: 'Rebuilt' RAF Langham from above showing the 'A' shape runways, 'spectacle loops' and the various dispersed buildings.

6. The ANZACs Come to Langham: 1944

On 1st March 1944, RAF Langham was back on active duty. Not only was it radically upgraded with three concrete runways and associated infrastructure; it was apparent from the start this was to be Langham's most prolific period of service, as 82 fliers were already posted there by the first day.

Over the coming weeks more and more personnel turned up – air and ground crews, medics, WAAFs, RAF Regiment. The skills of those arriving also gave the strongest indication of the heightened significance Langham's role was now taking. Intelligence officers, cyphers, plotters, signals, flight controllers, meteorologists were turning up daily – even a Chemical Warfare Adviser made a short visit as the threat of gas attack was still considered a possibility. Then, on 5th March, the man who was to assume command of the whole proceedings landed.

A charismatic character, Group Captain Arthur Edmund Clouston, DFC, AFC was a well-decorated and seasoned flier. Originally a Kiwi with a passion for the air, in 1930, already a keen pilot with any amount of flying hours under his belt, he confidently applied to join the Royal New Zealand Air Force. To his utter astonishment, his application was rejected. Being a small and sparsely funded, fledgling service at the time, it had no positions available. So passionate was he, that, with this news ringing in his ears and thoroughly irritated, he took the bull by the horns and moved halfway across the globe to the UK with hopes of enlisting with the RAF. Imagine his mood as he heard he was once more rejected. But this time on medical grounds – his blood pressure was too high. He couldn't believe it. Having passed every other test satisfactorily and now completely frustrated and downright exasperated, he was told to reapply in a month's time with advice in the meantime to ease himself gently into life in Britain.

One month later and the same result. Two months later still and rejection again, only this time he didn't need to be told. He could read the answer in the medical officer's face. Frustration now turned to desperation and he resorted to calling in some favours and managed to secure one last attempt. Explaining that he had been flying for some years back in New Zealand with absolutely no problems at all, he was allowed to go up in the back seat of a trainer to see how he coped. With an experienced pilot in the front seat performing all manner of extreme acrobatics, Clouston loved every minute. To the amazement of the medical officer who took his blood pressure the moment he landed, they found that his blood pressure was actually completely normal during flying than while awaiting medical examinations on the ground!

From that moment, he never looked back. In October 1930, at No. 3 Flying Training School, he went solo after only a few hours flying. By the Spring of 1931, he was a Pilot Officer with 25 Squadron. Soon he was selected as one of the team that performed formation aerobatics at the RAF Hendon display.

In a characteristically bold move, Clouston left the RAF in 1935 to become a test pilot at RAE Farnborough. Not content with that, in his spare time at Farnborough, Clouston competed in air racing and record-breaking. By 1938, he had established eleven records.

With the outbreak of war in 1939, Clouston re-joined the RAF, initially remaining as a test pilot back at Farnborough. Although the unit operated some high-speed fighters, it was surprisingly forbidden to arm their weapons. Undeterred, Clouston would chase any intruding German aircraft he encountered to scare them off. Later the orders on arming test flight aircraft changed and, on one occasion, Clouston claimed shooting down a Heinkel 111 and a Messerschmitt Bf 110 during the same test flight in a Spitfire.

In April 1941, he transferred to serve with 219 Squadron operating Bristol Beaufighters. His experience at Farnborough paid dividends. In reports he submitted to the Air Ministry, his suggestions pushed through improvements to the cannons on Beaufighters and better training for radar operators. By March 1943, Clouston was promoted to Wing Commander and posted to command 224 Squadron, operating Consolidated B-24 Liberators on anti-submarine operations. The Squadron repeatedly came under attack from the Luftwaffe. For his leadership and accomplishment in combat, Clouston was awarded the Distinguished Flying Cross in October 1943.

It was clear Clouston was made of the right stuff as a senior officer. Accordingly, in February 1944, he was promoted again, this time to Group Captain, awarded the Distinguished Service Order and subsequently posted as the new Station Commander of RAF Langham. He wasted no time in using his new-found position to get things done.

In a chapter of his autobiography, *The Dangerous Skies*, Clouston wrote: "The runways at Langham in Norfolk were still incomplete when I arrived." He was "irked" by what he saw as time wasted by some of the labourers. Nevertheless, he realised "that if I argued with them it would make matters worse, and I would be lucky to get away in one piece." He adopted a novel approach to resolve matters: "I took a large service camera and pretended to photograph them several times during a day. The manoeuvre succeeded. Work on the runways sped up".

One of his first duties as the Station Commander was to accept an inspection visit from Air Chief Marshal Sir William Sholto Douglas, who was the Air Officer Commander in Chief, Coastal Command no less. The A.O.C-in-C. was not alone either. Accompanying him was Air Vice Marshal Frank L. Hopps – Air Officer Commanding No 16 Group, of which Langham was now a part. This was a clear sign of the importance expected of the newly refurbished base and an indication of the unreserved high expectation placed on its new Station Commander.

The two dignitaries stayed for three hours which included lunch. There is no record of the satisfaction (or otherwise) of the visit, but it may have been rather underwhelming given the state of the runways and judging by the closing statement on the Operations Record Book for the month, worded in the typically impersonal service fashion of the time:

"Throughout the month difficulty was experienced by shortage of personnel and the unfinished state of the buildings. Particularly was this so in respect of the Officers' accommodation. For the first twenty days Officers were without batmen and as the weather was in the main wet and cold, a certain amount of discomfort was experienced, but was borne cheerfully by all.

"By the end of the month things were a little better. The new Airmens' and Sergeants' Messes had been occupied and found satisfactory; telephones were going in and most of the essential buildings could be occupied."

Obviously Clouston's challenge was going to be a significant one, but he was not about to be deterred or daunted.

As the number of service personnel steadily grew over the course of the next few weeks (hopefully including the influx of batmen to assuage the Officers' discomfort!) so too did the

capability of the Station that Clouston was to put to work. Of these new arrivals, the Station Commander was not the only antipodean – many, many more were on their way. During the month of April 1944, aircraft and members of 455 and 489 Squadrons steadily arrived from Leuchars in Scotland. These were made up of Australians and New Zealanders supplemented and mixed with some British service members. Over time, a small number of Canadians joined them and even a couple of Norwegians.

489 Squadron was a unit from New Zealand led by Wing Commander J. S. 'Johnny' Dinsdale, DFC. Although a Brit born in Christchurch, Dorset in 1913 and originally joined RAF in August 1938, he was transferred to RNZAF in January 1944. As such he was relatively new in post. By contrast 455 Squadron's commander was an experienced war pilot. 455 was an Australian outfit and their commanding officer, Wing Commander J. N. Davenport, DFC was an Aussie himself from New South Wales. Jack Davenport had been flying Handley Page Hampden bombers in raids on Germany and awarded the Distinguished Flying Cross in recognition of his leadership and operational skills. On promotion to Acting Wing Commander, he was appointed commanding officer of the squadron and oversaw their conversion from Hampden bombers to Beaufighters. As we'll see later, Davenport was to distinguish himself even further during his time at Langham. Both men

had their work cut out because they just had a matter of days to get their respective squadrons settled in before Clouston called them into action.

Only a month after his first visit with the A.O.C-in-C., Air Vice Marshal Hopps returned for another stopover to check on progress. He must have left with a very different impression on this occasion. Clouston had certainly got things moving. The base was now most assuredly operational, already running assault and reconnaissance sorties over the North Sea. All aircraft and personnel from both 455 and 489 Squadrons had arrived by 13th April. Only five days later, 489 Squadron flew its first sortie – a recce off the Dutch coast by four Beaufighters. That passed without incident but, at dawn the following morning, 455 Squadron also flew a similar op. This time, though, one of the aircraft, code sign 'UB-V' (which we'll hear about again later), spotted an enemy vessel. Eager to engage, the sighting was immediately radioed to base but this time it passed the details to RAF North Coates for them to respond. North Coates also had a Beaufighter Strike Wing and an attack was launched right away. Langham did not have long to wait for its share of action.

On the same day as Air Vice Marshal Hopps paid his second visit, 489 Squadron suffered its first casualties. Only a week after their arrival at Langham, pilot Flight Lieutenant Brindley Stourton and his navigator Flying Officer Robert White in their Beaufighter 'P6-W' failed to return from a reconnaissance mission along Dutch coast. Their bodies were recovered in occupied Holland and buried in Den Burg cemetery on the island of Texel just off the Dutch coast. They were not the last.

There is a stark contrast in the records of this period with those prior to the rebuild. For the twenty-four months of 1941 and 1942, the Accident Log for the station shows 20 entries with 20 crew members losing their lives. By comparison, within only the first six months of the station reopening, there were 43 aircraft recorded as having crashed and 43 airmen killed – that's more than double the deaths in a quarter of the time. Hardly a week went by without a member of 455 and 489 Squadrons not making it. With the squadrons dedicated to anti-shipping operations, many of the aircraft came to grief at sea. Consequently, a weighty number of the bodies of the aircrew were never retrieved. The names of those that were not recovered, including those from 455 and 489, are commemorated at the Runnymede Memorial.

The build-up of offensive operations from Langham was not random. There was a growing intensity across the whole of southern Britain in 1944. Under Operation Overlord, the Allies were amassing the biggest amphibious invasion force in history to retake the occupied countries of continental Europe. By mid-summer, everything, and everybody, was in place and the Allies were ready for what were to become the

momentous events of D-Day.

Despite being at a distance from the build-up on the south coast, Langham did its bit. In the air and on the ground, the crews saw no let up. While in the month of April 1944, the Operations Log recorded 285 flying hours on operations with 483 hours of training, in May those figures almost doubled with 640 on ops and 715 training. The level of operational sorties had progressively heated up as attacks multiplied on German resource convoys running along the Dutch coast, squeezing Germany's ability to support its war effort by hitting its supply lines. The additional training sorties were to hone formation skills and practice runs of torpedo attacks and bomb dropping. The purpose soon came clear. Langham was about to play its part in Overlord.

Everyone knew that D-Day was coming. But when? Where? As June 1944 approached, armed patrols switched from the North Sea to the French coast. Now they knew it was going to be soon. There had been a couple of patrols sent to the north coast of France earlier in May, but the focus was still on the North Sea convoys. That was until the last week of May, when operational sorties suddenly stopped. Then on 30th, eleven 489 Squadron Beaufighters were ordered to patrol-sweep the area between Cherbourg and Le Harve. A few days later,

Left: Crews and officers from 489 Squadron pictured in April 1944.

just before dawn at 04:02 hours on 2nd June, yet another eleven aircraft were despatched, drawn from both 455 and 489 Squadrons, this time to rendezvous with a squadron of Spitfires just off Beachy Head and conduct an anti-E-Boat patrol between Barfleur (about 12 miles east of Cherbourg) and Dieppe.

The very next day, 3rd June, 03:56 hours, twelve aircraft, six from each squadron, met up with a squadron of Spitfires also at Beachy Head, sweeping from Dieppe to the west of Cherbourg. Without realising it at the time, what those young men had done was something truly momentous. They had just cleared the area for the D-Day landings.

The loss of fellow aircrew was fairly commonplace for the Langham Squadrons and felt keenly. Also on that day, 'A' Flight of 489 Squadron crucially lost their commander. Squadron Leader Stanley Kellow, DFC was tragically killed – not on an operational sortie but, with wretched misfortune, on a training flight. And it was doubly tragic as, not only was he a well-respected commander, he had led his crews valiantly, himself surviving a number of intrepid torpedo attacks on enemy convoys and now his crews were facing D-Day operations without him. Kellow was only a passenger offering instruction to the crew when the engine of Beaufighter 'P6-A' cut out on approach, stalled and crashed, killing all on board. Wing Commander D. H. 'Hammy' Hammond, a bank clerk from

Christchurch, took his place (in the picture on p66 above, he is standing third from the right). Such challenges facing the squadrons were constant and were not about to let up.

Because it was such a closely guarded secret, the crews didn't know that they were patrolling the precise location of what was to become the Normandy beachhead. The 5th June 1944 was the original planned day for the invasion force to set sail across the Channel[13]. That day, Group Captain Clouston received orders[14] that his station was to be placed on "immediate readiness" with twelve fully armed aircraft loaded with bombs to be on ten minutes availability night and day. On a normal operation, aircraft would take much longer from crew boarding to getting in the air[15]. The implications of such orders were not lost on anyone at the Station from admin staff to aircrew.

On 6th June, those twelve 'on alert' Beaufighters were sat in readiness at the end of one of the runways. To ensure a quick getaway within the mandated ten minutes, the crews were billeted in a mobile caravan that had been parked next to the runway. The weather was fair with a bit of cloud and the occasional shower. To while away the time, the mixed crews of Aussies, Kiwis and Brits were relaxing quietly, some reading, some chatting together, some enjoying a game of cards. Just another day. Then a little before 8am…

SCRAMBLE!!!

Their calm relaxation was suddenly and swiftly turned into furious commotion. The crews flung down their papers and cards, grabbed their gear and raced to the waiting planes. They were in the air in a matter of minutes.

In no time, each pilot had manoeuvred into formation heading out to sea away to the east. Meanwhile their navigators in the rear seat had received their orders via radio to set course for RAF Manston in Kent. The formation turned south. Less than an hour later, they were greeted by an extraordinary sight as they made their approach. The airfield was an outright swarm of British and American military aircraft of all varieties. Planes were taking off and landing in constant quick succession. Guided in by the Air Traffic Controller, the Langham boys managed to land quickly and found an unoccupied corner of the aerodrome to park. After disembarking, they caught up with crews from countless other bases all gathered around a radio listening to the BBC broadcasting news of the events across the Channel. The atmosphere, a jittery cocktail of excitement and apprehension, was palpable. D-Day was on!

As it turned out, they were not called into further action on that fateful day. Despite the anti-climax, it left an enduring imprint in the memories of those crews. Later the next day,

Right: Rockbeaus of 455 Squadron ready to take to the skies.

they were ordered on patrols along the Belgian coast and reported a few skirmishes with German E-boats but nothing of particular significance before being recalled to Langham. In the weeks that followed, both squadrons returned to patrol the Normandy skies in protection of the seemingly endless mass of military hardware and troops that poured into the beachheads now secured in France. Just another day. Just another set of sorties. Just another episode in a war where the Langham crews did their bit.

With all this feverish increase in operations, it is no surprise, then, that the ANZAC period threw up many accounts of both bravery and tragedy. One such story concerns Beaufighter TFX, code 'UB-E' of 455 Squadron.

The Beaufighter was a fast, powerful, multi-role fighter. Its size allowed it to carry heavy armament and weapons without major performance penalties – receiving the nicknames *Rockbeau* for its use as a rocket-armed attack aircraft and *Torbeau* as a torpedo bomber (hence the TFX short for Torpedo Fighter Mark X) in attacking enemy shipping. These were the main roles assigned to the Beaufighters stationed at Langham. Lloyd Wiggins, one of the Flight Commanders of 455 Squadron, said:

"The Beaufighter was a beautiful aircraft, smooth as silk and with no vices. It... withstood a lot of punishment." [16]

It needed to. The Beaufighter Strike Wings fought up close and personal.

With the potent introduction of the Beaufighter, assault tactics on convoys were radically transformed. The swift, single fighter get-in-get-out attacks continued but, for larger merchant convoys with escorts, a new approach came in with deadly force – the mass attack. These combined wings of up to forty, or occasionally fifty, aircraft usually included *Rockbeaus* and *Torbeaus* accompanied by cannon-armed anti-flak Beaufighters and an escort of Mustangs. The strategy opened with the approach. After sighting the convoy, the *Torbeaus* would break off, taking a wider sweep and timing their approach just behind the rest of the wing. The strike would begin with the initial wave of anti-flaks and *Rockbeaus* in a relatively shallow dive, but at full power, from about 1,500 feet. The pilots would pick out one specific escort vessel each, firing at frighteningly close range to the waterline of the vessel and not pulling out until mast height [17]. As well as causing significant damage, this would instil maximum panic in the convoy vessels and sent their protective formation scattering – although the more experienced German captains were a touch canny and often held their defensive position.

Right: Beaufighter Pilot's cockpit.

Then the second wave. With perfect timing from their wider sweep, the *Torbeaus* settled into a line astern formation to begin with, starting their run as the *Rockbeaus* and anti-flaks were dispersing. Then, manoeuvring into 'fluid pairs', they came in very low at wave top height and targeted the larger merchant vessels, now less protected by the scattering escorts, waiting till the last second to release their torpedoes[18]. The navigators, peering to the rear out of the dorsal gun cupola, would scan the scene hoping to see a direct hit before the pilots of all aircraft would hit the power, get as fast and low as possible, weaving and skimming the waves until they were clear. Once free from the possibility of counter-attack, it was time to gain height, ease off the throttle and head for home.

Needless to say, this technique proved very effective but came with extremely high-risk.

'UB-E' in the photograph (right) was flown by pilot Flight Sgt (later Pilot Officer) Norman Steer from Prospect, South Australia and his navigator/gunner Flying Officer Basil Roberts from Townsville, Queensland.

On the morning of 13th August 1944, Norman and Basil took off in 'UB-E' as part of a combined operation of approximately 30 aircraft made up of squadrons from Langham, Bircham Newton, North Coates and Coltishall to attack a German convoy of 15 ships that had been spotted off the Dutch coast.

Similar to most of these encounters, the attack was intense and furious with the heavily armed ships defending for their lives. Nevertheless, the air attack was pressed home and five of the ships were left burning. In the ferocity of battle, Norman and Basil's aircraft had been hit by flak but somehow, they managed to limp back home only to 'belly land' because the hydraulics had failed so 'UB-E' couldn't lower its undercarriage. Despite the fact that the aircraft was severely damaged with the No 2 engine completely ripped off in the crash, amazingly both crewmen survived unharmed.

Regardless of their ordeal, Norman and Basil were back flying equally dangerous ops again. Only a few months later, on 15th October 1944, now flying aircraft 'UB-V' (that we heard about above), they took off with five other Beaufighters of 455 Squadron on a recce. Just off the West Frisian Islands, the squadron sighted four German vessels and attacked, badly damaging all four ships. But once again during the heat of battle, they were hit. This time though their luck had changed. They were forced to ditch 'UB-V' in the sea. Some of the other crews on the mission saw Norman and Basil getting in their dinghy and briefed their Squadron Commander once back at Langham. A broadcast was put out to the enemy in the hopes that they would be picked up as POWs. We do not know whether the Germans responded but we do know the dinghy

Right: Bristol Beaufighter TFX 'UB-E' of 455 Squadron, circa May 1944.

was not found and, sadly, neither pilot nor navigator survived.

Like many other aircrews, having got away with one harrowing attack, undaunted, they put their lives on the line time and again knowing only too well the dangers they were facing. These two men from the other side of the world paid the ultimate price. The body of Flying Officer Roberts was found floating in the sea off the Norwegian coast hundreds of miles north of where they ditched. He was buried in Risor Civil Cemetery, south Norway. He was only 20 years old. Pilot Officer Steer, who was a squadron 'oldie' at just 29, was never found.

It's a tragic irony that these two young Aussies at one turn found themselves in their trusty but wounded Beaufighter heading home to crash land and emerge without a scratch, only at the next turn to meet a similar fate but this time discover their luck had run out.

During the ANZACs time at Langham, the most notable event – certainly the most celebrated, as it was later reported in the national press – came on 21st July, 1944. Being the height

Left: Beaufighters in a mass attack on a German convoy – note the rockets hitting the water.
Right: Basil Roberts (right) and Norman Steer (left) with stripes on his arm showing he was still a Sergeant at the time of the photograph, probably taken in mid-summer 1944.

of summer, it was another fine day. Sunny, a few clouds building and where would the British summer be without the occasional shower of rain? The crews on standby were relaxing in the crew room – a few sat reading, playing cards or a game of Shove Ha'penny on the table. Some were outside in the warm, cooled by a slight breeze and dodging the odd, random shower.

A little after 10:30am, a single Beaufighter from 489 Squadron went out on a recce across the North Sea toward Heligoland Bight. At first, nothing else spoilt the air of leisureliness. Towards lunchtime, more crews were reporting to the crew room and the atmosphere elevated. Interest really began to change when some of the crews that should have been off duty that day were ordered to report in. When twenty-one Beaufighters from the Strike Wing at RAF Strubby in Lincolnshire suddenly broke the calm and landed at the airfield, the excitement was palpable.

The tension grew over the whole day until late in the afternoon, all the crews from the combined squadrons were called to the Ops Room for a briefing. They were to attack the largest German convoy of the war so far – approximately 40 ships in all. Reports vary in numbers but, by 20:00 hrs that evening, an attack force of between 40 and 50 Beaufighters – *Rockbeaus*, *Torbeaus* and anti-flaks – from 455 and 489 Squadrons from Langham and 144 and 404 Squadrons from Strubby took off and headed out to sea.

An hour and ten minutes later, the massive formation made its final course correction by turning to starboard and heading south toward the German coast. It was a matter of only a few minutes before the convoy appeared before them through the late evening haze. The airmen were utterly astonished by what they saw. The briefing had nowhere near prepared them to see the scale of the convoy – vessels as far as the eye could see in the fading summer light. Surprise quickly abated however, and all attention soon returned to sharp focus on the business at hand. Employing the now very familiar, tried and tested assault tactics of the mass attack described above,

the first wave dived toward the escorts followed swiftly by the second wave of *Torbeaus*. The attack was relentless. One anti-flak aircraft was seen attacking an escort vessel, then making a short climb only to dive again spraying another ship with canon fire and unbelievably repeated the stunt on yet a third!

The adrenalin rush amongst the crews was pumping at a rate of knots almost as fast as the speed of Beaufighters themselves and yet the whole attack lasted a relatively short time. From the photographs and films taken by the squadrons, the assault inflicted total carnage. Impressively, despite the massive size of the convoy, every single vessel across the whole flotilla suffered some damage, mostly severe with many either listing or sinking with great plumes of dark smoke and fire belching across all quarters of the vessels. And what was even more astonishing was the fact that, in the face of heavy defensive fire from the German shipping, all the Beaufighters returned home. The last planes landed around midnight.

If the story above was the most notable, the following is probably the most poignant. It concerns two brothers from Australia whose fates were incredibly and heartbreakingly entwined.

Born in Tasmania just over 18 months apart in the early 1920s, Henry James Brock (the older brother) and Harold Eric Brock (the younger) grew up in the Derwent Valley, Central

Highlands region where their parents, Harold Snr. and Jean, had established significant farming estates.

Too young to join up when war broke out, the brothers continued farming on the family estates until they were able to enlist. Henry was first to join up at Hobart in 1941, followed by Harold in 1942. Both joined the Royal Australian Air Force. As chance would have it, their respective journeys brought them both to RAF Langham.

Harold, pictured overleaf, qualified as a navigator and was posted to 455 Squadron in April 1944 flying Beaufighters on numerous operations from Langham attacking enemy shipping in the North Sea. On 10th August 1944, both 455 and 489 Squadrons were on a mission off the Dutch coast. The sortie was a successful one in terms of the damage inflicted on a German convoy attacked just off Wangerooge, the eastern-most of the Frisian Islands. Not so successful though was that four of the aircraft failed to return, three from 455 Squadron and one from 489.

On 12th August his mother received the letter opposite, signed by Wing Commander Jack Davenport, the Squadron Commander.

Just two months later, on 11th October 1944, by an uncanny twist of fate, Harold's older brother, Henry, now a pilot in the

Right: On 12th August Harold's mother received this letter, signed by Wing Commander Jack Davenport, the Squadron Commander.

No. 455 Squadron, R.A.A.F.,
Royal Air Force Station,
Langham.
Norfolk.

Ref:- 4558/140/105/P.1.   12th August, 1944.

Dear Mrs. Brock,

I deeply regret to confirm that your son, AUS.408396 Flight Sergeant H.E. Brock, is missing and believed to have lost his life in operations on the evening of the 10th August, 1944.

Your son was the Navigator/Wireless Operator of an aircraft detailed for an important operation off the coast of Holland, in company with other aircraft from this Station. A very determined and courageous attack was carried out against the enemy off the Frisian Islands, and it was immediately after this attack that the aircraft was observed to crash into the sea. They would have been killed instantly.

Flight Sergeant Brock joined this Squadron at the end of April this year, and since that time he had been very busy and had completed outstanding work, both training and on operations. His ability and keenness were always evident, and this, backed by determination and sound common-sense, made him a popular and valuable member of the Squadron. We shall all miss him very much indeed.

His brother, Flying Officer H.J. Brock, has also been informed.

His personal belongings will, in the course of a few days, be sent, as regulations require, to the Standing Committee of Adjustment, Colnbrook, Slough, Bucks., the department which deals with the effects of missing airmen. These will then be forwarded to you as soon as possible, but you will understand that the shipping position makes delays inevitable.

I would like to express and extend to you my sincere personal sympathy and also that of every member of the Squadron.

If I can help you in any way, or if there is any further information I can give, you have only to let me know.

Yours sincerely,

Wing Commander, Commanding,
No. 455 Squadron, R.A.A.F.

RAAF, was also posted to 455 Squadron. Still stationed at RAF Langham and still equipped with Beaufighter TFXs, he flew at least one operation from here before the Squadron was transferred to Dallachy in Scotland.

On 26th February 1945, Henry was sent on a similar mission as Harold out over the North Sea to search for any stray German convoys. Again, like his brother, his aircraft didn't return. He was posted as missing in the vicinity of Saint Fergus Aberdeenshire, Scotland. The following day with no sign of the aircraft he was presumed dead by Operational Headquarters.

The families of those serving with the armed forces dreaded receiving official mailings in the post. Such letters would most often mean only one thing. Mrs Brock's heart must have sunk to the floor when, 12,000 miles away, she received yet a second letter of condolence in February 1945 telling her that her surviving son, Henry, met almost the exact same fate as her younger son. So far from home in a war she didn't ask for and a place she hadn't heard of.

Even the Squadron Commanders were caught up in events. Within a month of having had the unfortunate duty of writing

Right: Flight Sergeant Harold Eric Brock in front of his Beaufighter, smiling happily, unaware of his impending fate.
Far Right: Arming a 489 Squadron Beaufighter with 20mm cannon rounds.

to Mrs Brock about her son, Wing Commander Jack Davenport was about to show why he was so admired by his crews.

As was his custom when not flying, Davenport was in the control tower on the evening of 9th September 1944 watching out for his crews coming home. It had been a long day. There had already been ten reconnaissance flights throughout the day, the first setting off at a quarter to five in the morning. Nearly twelve hours later, the eleventh flight took off – a single 455 Squadron Beaufighter, 'UB-J', with two Aussies, Flying Officers Bill Stanley and Ken Dempsey, performing yet another recce off the Dutch coast. After an hour and twenty minutes, they spotted a convoy which promptly opened fire on them hitting their port engine. Dempsey reported back to base that they'd suffered an engine failure and were heading home. The alert went out to air sea rescue units in case they ditched on the way and the ambulance and fire crews on the ground were put on standby.

Somehow getting the wounded aircraft back to Norfolk, pilot Bill Stanley was struggling to keep his Beaufighter on a direct approach with the starboard engine trying

Left: Beaufighter 'UB-L' was the aircraft Ft Sgt H E Brock was flying in when he was killed.

Pilot Officer Henry James Brock.

Wing Commander Jack Davenport.

to pull the aircraft in one direction and he fighting to correct the yaw with full rudder in the other. Having been fighting with the controls all the way home, he just couldn't manage it anymore. As he forced a landing, the undercarriage collapsed. The plane spun round in a ground-loop and burst into flames. Seeing this, Davenport instantly ran down to his car and sped across the airfield to the scene.

Dempsey immediately jumped clear of the inferno from the rear canopy, but Bill Stanley was trapped. The impact had pushed the instrument panel back into the cockpit and jammed his boots fast. Just then the fuel tanks burst and ignited the unspent ammunition. With flames and shells going off in all directions, Davenport ordered everyone to stand clear. Then to everyone's horror, completely ignoring his own instructions, he dashed onto the wing and mounted the fuselage to force the forward canopy open. The cockpit was engulfed by now and, grabbing hold of Stanley, Davenport heaved at Bill's confined torso. In the same instant, the body of the Beaufighter collapsed jolting the two airmen viciously. Summoning up as much strength as he could, Jack tugged again at Bill, this time managing to pull him out of his snagged boots and dragged him clear to a waiting ambulance.

Jack suffered burns to his head, hands and legs while Bill was in a bad way, severely and extensively scorched. Unbelievably, despite the agonising pain, Bill insisted on completing the mission and, while laid in the ambulance, began reporting details of the convoy he and Ken had spotted.

Bill Stanley had several operations and, after some time, recovered in the local hospital. Meanwhile Jack Davenport healed relatively quickly and was subsequently awarded the George Medal for his actions.

In early September 1944, 280 Squadron returned for a month, this time flying Vickers Warwick Air Sea Rescue Mk1s partly to support the Arnhem invasion. The Warwick was a larger version of the better known Wellington, both designed by Sir Barnes Wallis, the man that developed the famous bouncing bomb used in the Dam Busters raid. The air sea rescue version of the Warwick had the bomb bay converted so as to carry a lifeboat fitted with parachutes. When the crew spotted survivors in the sea, they dropped the boat as close as possible to float down to a gentle landing in the water. The survivors could then swim to the boat, erect the folded down mast, raise the sail and navigate back to shore.

It was just as well 280 Squadron had arrived since they were called to rescue the Langham aircrew of Beaufighter 'P6-E' of 489 Squadron who endured the most extraordinary rescue incident on the days and nights following 2nd/3rd October 1944.

Among the worst letters received by the families of service personnel were those that reported their loved ones 'missing in action'. Having their fate left open and unresolved kept the families in unbearable limbo. Two such letters were sent to the families of Pilot Warrant Officer Douglas Mann, from Greymouth New Zealand, and his navigator Flight Sergeant Donald Kennedy, a Brit from Southport, Lancashire.

Their luck was precarious right from the start. To begin with, they weren't even supposed to be flying that night. As chance would have it, one of the pilots of the six Beaufighters due to go out on what was intended to be a routine night-time shipping recce fell ill. With the last few embers of 2nd October fading away, the six Beaufighters took off at five minute intervals starting at 23:30hrs, with Duggie and Don finding themselves the second aircraft to get away.

The weather was patchy that night, the fine afternoon having given way to cloud and eventually occasional showers. The flight out across the North Sea was in and out of cloud. Four of the aircraft found nothing, but, for the other two, as often happened on these flights, the routine quietude rudely switched into adrenalin-pumping action. At around 01:40 hrs, one of the Beaufighters launched an attack on a convoy they had spotted. Coming across the convoy themselves, Duggie and Don joined in, dropping down low to line up for a torpedo run.

The low cloud had thickened considerably by now and Duggie was struggling to see. Determined but unsure of his heading, he pressed on. Then disaster. Out of nowhere something long and thin suddenly appeared out of the gloom directly ahead. Instinctively, he pulled at the column to get out of its path. Too late. The starboard wing hit the object and tore violently at the aircraft. The aircraft veering in all directions, Duggie fought with the controls. He somehow managed to keep the plane flying, but the convoy was now firing everything it had at them.

But worse was to come. With barely enough speed to stay airborne, Duggie turned the stricken Beaufighter in order to escape the shellfire. As he did so, from the rear canopy, Don spotted a problem. The collision had ruptured one of their fuel tanks. He shouted to Duggie that they were gushing petrol in gallons. That was it – the plane was done for. They had no option but to ditch in the drink.

Badly bruised and battered but thankfully still alive, they clambered into their dinghies. They were wet and cold and to make matters worse, the fierce wind was whipping up the sea into a heavy swell adding to their discomfort. The morning brought a measure of calm but also catastrophe. The rations in one of the dinghies had been lost through a tear in the fabric floor. But this wasn't to be their only stroke of misfortune on that initial day.

First there was elation. Their hopes were raised of a rescue when two US fighter planes spotted them and dropped a flare to mark their position. As chance would have it, the crew of a ditched US Boeing B-17 Flying Fortress had also been spotted not that far away. In an outrageous turn of bad luck, the rescue aircraft, from Bircham Newton, dropped a lifeboat for the Fortress crew and, assuming the two sighting were one and the same, headed home satisfied they had saved the day. Duggie and Don were on their own again. As the hours ticked by, the realisation of no rescue dawned on them and elation turned to despair.

Days went by and what little water and rations they had were gone. Back in Langham, with no sign of Duggie and Don, they were presumed dead so no air-sea searches were sent to look for them. None of the routine patrols that did go out in the first few days came across them. Five days after their crash, they were cold, wet, starving and totally disoriented. Suddenly, a combined wing of Beaufighters and Mustangs heading for the Dutch coast flew toward them at low level and top speed. Hardly had they roused themselves from their weakened state than the planes were gone. Thoroughly dejected, they slumped back into the dinghy.

Then their luck changed. Two air sea rescue Warwicks from Langham spotted the dinghies and dropped one of their Lindholme lifeboats[19] which landed about 300 yards away from Duggie and Don. The rescue aircraft circled for some time surprised that no attempt was made to get to the lifeboat until they realised that the two stricken airmen must be in trouble. They then dropped another lifeboat taking extra care to get it as close as possible to the dinghies. Summoning up the last of his strength, Duggie managed to reach the boat and pull Don's dinghy alongside. They took on water and rations so as to bolster their exhausted bodies as the Warwick, low on fuel, headed back to Langham.

Later that day another Warwick was sent out but, by the time they found them, it was getting dark and the rescuers, unable to help, had to abandon Duggie and Don once again. Then the pendulum of luck that had been swinging back and forth

since they took off five days ago swayed out of their favour to thwart them even further. Yet another Warwick, searching late that night for a ditched bomber crew about five miles north of their position, was shot down. The next morning all air sea rescue missions were focused on finding the Warwick crew. Meanwhile Duggie and Don, utterly exhausted and dejected, drifted aimlessly across the North Sea.

Over the next three days, the threat of enemy attack and bad weather out on the North Sea hampered further attempts at sighting the beleaguered airmen despite the fact that other crews were sighted and rescued. By now Duggie and Don's lifeboat had drifted approximately 50 miles south west of their last known position. Weak and wet through, they had lost all hope of rescue.

That did not deter the Air Sea Rescue crews from scanning the waves for the Beaufighter men. Indeed some of the Beaufighter crews themselves joined the search at the same time providing air cover for the Warwicks in case they were to fall under attack from any of the marauding fighters of the Luftwaffe. Neither did it prevent the high speed launches (HSLs) of the RAF's Air Sea Rescue Marine Craft Unit from setting out to sea in the hope of receiving a radio call from an

Right: An air-sea rescue Vickers Warwick carrying a lifeboat in the specially adapted bomb bay.

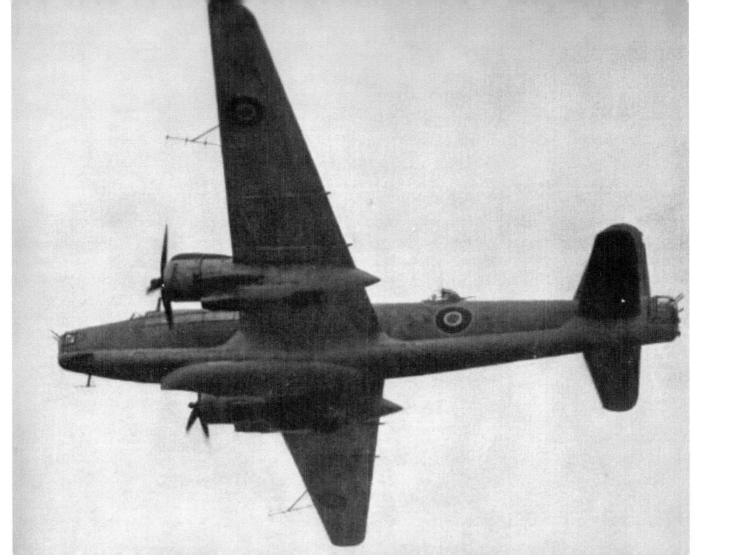

air crew. One such vessel, *HSL2679*, out on patrol in the North Sea on 10th October received such a call at noon from an ASR Hudson of 279 Squadron out of Bircham Newton. Immediately the Duty Officer on board ordered *HSL2679* to make for the coordinates radioed to them and called back to the Hudson to circle the dinghy so, as they approached the area, the aircraft above would provide a clear marker to guide them in. By some miracle it was Duggie and Don. But they were so emaciated the launch crew had to haul them out of the dinghy. Once they were back on dry land, they were taken immediately to the naval hospital in Great Yarmouth and telegrams were sent to the families correcting the men's status from 'missing' to 'safe'.

At last fickle fortune had swung their way and the ordeal was over.

By now, as the summer of 1944 had given way to autumn, the Allies were making significant advances across Europe. The German garrison in Paris had surrendered in August and, on the Eastern Front, the Russian forces had made similar gains as they surged into Crimea and Romania. By mid-October the Allied army entered Germany for the first time. Hitler's response was to mark a desperate and terrifying turning point in modern warfare. He ordered the launch of the so-called

Left: Kennedy and Mann about to be rescued by HSL2679.

'vengeance weapons'. The unmanned V-1 'Doodlebug' aircraft and the lethal V-2 ballistic missile struck fear into the hearts of those living in Britain.

At one stage, over a hundred V-1s a day were fired on the southeast of England. Altogether, more than 9,500 reached these shores. The Allied advances in France finally halted the V-1 campaign as the last launch site in range of Britain was overrun. Attacks by the V-2 rockets however were unaffected. Launched from sites across the North Sea in Holland, the first V-2 rockets reached East Anglia in late summer. In response, bombing raids from Norfolk airfields attacked V-2 launch sites.

Locally on a lighter note, with the tide of the war heading eastward across Europe, the time was right for signposts, taken down earlier in the war (so as to hinder any German advances if there was an invasion), to be put back across Norfolk. Better yet, the ban on coastal access was partially lifted to offer some respite to the local population. It wasn't all good news though – some local pubs went dry as beer ran out in a number of places!

With the Axis Powers now in retreat on all fronts, October saw the next significant change in the operations at Langham. On 19th the station commander received a notification by signal from Coastal Command Headquarters that both ANZAC Squadrons were to transfer to RAF Dallachy, Scotland. He issued the Movement Order the following day.

The year 1944 was unquestionably *the* decisive year of the war. Even at the time, there was a general sense that the war was, at last, there to be won by the Allies. The ANZAC's period at Langham, though relatively brief, was also of the greatest intensity that the airfield experienced in all its years of service. In no small part owing to the daring and effective exploits of 455 and 489 Squadrons and the devastating loses they inflicted, by August 1944, the Germans had stopped daytime convoys along the eastern stretches of the North Sea coast. It was no particular surprise, then, that the ANZAC's time at Langham was now coming to a close.

It's true, 455 and 489 Squadrons had, in the end, played no active part in the D-Day landings or the ensuing offensive to drive the occupying forces back to Germany. Nevertheless, what is clear is that, had they not inflicted such overwhelming poundings on the North Sea convoys, German war industry would have been in a much greater position to supply and reinforce the defending armies in France. It's fair to say, then, that their fortitude and sacrifice will have saved the lives of thousands of Allied lives in that summer of 1944.

Compared to the headline grabbing exploits of Bomber Command and Fighter Command, the Strike Wings of Coastal Command rarely featured in the press of the day. Indeed, during the war, few people even knew that the Strike Wings existed. And yet few can doubt the outstanding commitment, determination and proficiency of these crews, many of whom came to this quiet part of the world from such distant shores. Many of whom too did not go home. At least some of their stories are kept alive in these pages and on the walls of the Langham Dome Museum.

With the convoys switching to night-time sailings and the departure of 455 and 489 Squadrons, the next chapter in Langham's wartime story brought in a new set of intrepid fliers, who similarly continued to deliver remarkable episodes of courage and sacrifice so maintaining the stranglehold on German supply lines established by the Beaufighter squadrons. In complete contrast to those who came to fight so bravely from the other side of the world, the next few months were also particularly memorable for bringing a local boy back home, one who acquitted himself in rather spectacular fashion.

7. Coming Home - The Road to Victory: 1945

Although the potent fighting force of the ANZAC Beaufighters had departed, the outstanding acts of endeavour remained. In yet another variation in the diverse set of squadrons operating from the airfield, 521 Meteorological Squadron arrived with Gloster Gladiators, Lockheed Venturas and Hudsons, Flying Fortresses and Hawker Hurricanes. These crews would fly out, usually without escort, to test weather conditions in the skies over enemy target areas before operational missions took off. It was very much a case for these fliers of get in, get the readings and get the hell out!

However, the most significant change came with the arrival of 612 Squadron, equipped with Wellington GRXIVs, a new variant bristling with electronics designed to detect and attack U-boats and E-Boats – the latter being fast, surface-raider gunships armed with torpedoes looking to attack Allied shipping in the North Sea. And 612 Squadron's arrival was especially poignant for one of their officers, a certain Flight Lieutenant J. N. B. Rounce.

In an odd turn of fate, Jeffrey Noel Bartram Rounce was born in Binham, barely a stone's throw from his new posting, only two miles to the south-west of the airfield at Langham. Growing up in this peaceful, picturesque rural settlement with the church and ruins of a Benedictine Priory dating back to the 11th Century, Jeff could never have imagined what lay in store.

That said, his ambitions had always been directed skyward. As a youngster, he so fancied the notion and excitement of flight that he built any number of model aircraft. Not surprising then that, one morning in the early summer of 1940, he took himself off to Norwich, found a recruiting office and promptly volunteered for service. With his sights set on becoming a pilot, he passed all the necessary tests and joined the RAF in June, aged just nineteen.

Alas, there was an obstacle. He discovered that because of the considerable numbers joining the RAF, there were only a few, much sought-after places on the pilot training course. Determined to fulfil his dreams, he took a slight detour. Hearing it to be a means of achieving a 'fast track' to flight training, he joined the Aerodrome Defence Corps (later renamed the RAF Regiment) and subsequently endured a brief tour of duty guarding Bomber Command aircraft at RAF Dishforth, Yorkshire. He did not have much longer to wait for his opportunity to fly. In the autumn of 1940, he was posted to Canada to train as a pilot under the Commonwealth Air Training Plan. A few short months later, he received his wings and three stripes with the rank of Sergeant Pilot. Toward the end of November 1941, Jeff was posted to 502 Squadron (Coastal

Command) at RAF Limavady,[20] Northern Ireland, where he flew Armstrong Whitworth Whitleys on anti-submarine ops.

Anti-shipping operations came to define his RAF career. By July 1942, he received a commission and promoted to Pilot Officer, whereupon he was posted to RAF Chivenor in Devon. Still with Coastal Command, he upgraded to the latest version of the Wellington, fitted with the newly developed ASV (air-to-surface vessel) radar and the innovative, retractable Leigh Light[21] – a powerful 22 million candlepower searchlight designed to illuminate the surface of the sea and any vessels, including submarines caught on the surface. This, too, was going to play a crucial part in Jeff's future.

After flying many missions in various theatres across Europe, in late 1944, Jeff was on active duty with 612 Squadron and, to his surprise and good fortune, found himself back home in Norfolk.

Above: Flight Sgt Jeff Rounce pictured sometime before he received his commission.

His mother, Miriam, was no doubt delighted to see him. Yet his presence also came with concern as she knew that on many nights he would be flying into unknown danger. Jeff came up with an ingenious solution to offer her some reassurance. As she still lived in the family home only a few miles from the base, when he took off around dusk, he would break off from the rest of the squadron and fly low over her house, so she knew he was out on a mission. Then on his return, before landing, he would repeat the breakaway fly-by, so setting her mind at rest that he was back safe and sound.

Being a local boy also made Jeff very popular with his fellow fliers. On occasion, he invited them to join him on a visit to his mother where they were treated to tea and cake. Come Christmas, those who were especially privileged did not sit down at the Mess but enjoyed their Christmas dinner at Mrs Rounce's! Miriam enjoyed these occasions and her son made her so proud, especially so when he was awarded the DFC.

It was 23rd January 1945. Jeff went out on a mission in Wellington '8W-E' across the North Sea where his radio operator picked up a signal on the ASV – a flotilla of six German E-Boats bent on attacking any Allied shipping supplying and defending the East Coast. Jeff immediately turned to attack and, as they approached, deployed the Leigh Light catching the E-boats in its glare. He pressed home the attack on four of the vessels damaging all of them. For most sorties, this would have been deemed to be a highly successful mission and the crew would have turned for home with a self-congratulatory pat on the back for a job well done. Not Jeff. Under fire, he came around and delivered the same fate to the other two E-boats.

Jeff's heroics were instantly recognised and his award of the DFC was marked by a citation in the London Gazette, 13th March 1945 which read:

"Flight Lieutenant Jeffrey Noel Bartram ROUNCE (129949), R.A.F.V.R., 612 Sqn. Since commencing a second tour of operational duty, this officer has participated in several attacks on enemy shipping. In January, 1945, Flight Lieutenant Rounce engaged 4 E-boats. In spite of considerable anti-aircraft fire, he pressed home a good bombing attack and afterwards came down to a low level to spray the two remaining vessels with machine gun fire. Some days later Flight Lieutenant Rounce made another good attack on a force of 4 E-boats. This officer has displayed high powers of leadership and has set a fine example of keenness and efficiency."

As the Germans had changed their strategy of convoy movement to night-time, shorter distance, port-to-port 'hopping', so too the assault tactics of Coastal Command changed. No longer the mass attack, this was the period of the Gilbey order of battle. Operation Gilbey was the name given to night-time anti-shipping actions launched by No. 16 Group of RAF Coastal Command against German vessels off the coast of the Netherlands.

When the skies were clear and the moon was out, the bomb-laden Wellingtons would go out singly about 15 minutes apart, each scanning a particular area for 'targets of opportunity'. Sometimes single *Torbeaus* would join in. On cloudy nights, though, the Wellingtons would also carry up to seventy flares. If a convoy was spotted, the radio operator would signal the location to HQ and the pilot would shadow the convoy from about ten miles distance. Meanwhile *Torbeaus* would be directed to the location by HQ. Once all the aircraft had rendezvoused, the Wellington would drop a series of flares, first to indicate the position and direction the convoy was sailing then a set to the landward side so the convoy was silhouetted against the coastline. The effect was to light up the convoy almost as if it were daytime. The ensuing combined attack would begin with the Wellington dropping its bombs from above and the *Torbeaus* releasing their torpedoes at low level. The exposed convoys had simply nowhere to hide.

With the daring attacks by the ANZAC Beaufighters and now the night-time raids by the Wellingtons, the latter twelve months of the war meant the German convoys knew no respite from the attacks mounted by Langham aircraft. This

stranglehold on German war industry dramatically reduced the capacity of the German fighting forces to replace the equipment losses it sustained as the Allies marched steadily across occupied Europe. It massively contributed to the restoration of peace in Europe, yet was given little column inches in the media at the time – nor indeed is it recognised widely in modern accounts of the period. Little wonder the men and women of Coastal Command referred to themselves as the 'Cinderella Service'.

Not all of the bravery on display at Langham came from the aircrews – or the men for that matter. On one rather dull, wet night in March 1945, Leading Aircraftwoman Ivy Cross was on duty. It had been a rather busy day starting at first light with numerous sorties taking off – some Hurricanes on 'THUM' Met flights, Fortresses doing 'RHOMBUS' sorties and Wellingtons on 'box' patrols. In the middle of the night at 01:48hrs, Wellington '7R-F' of 524 Squadron was taking off on a 'Percolate' Target Illumination patrol when one of its engines failed. The aircraft immediately crashed and burst into flames.

Ivy saw the flames through the gloom and leapt into her van, driving as fast as she could across the fields to the scene. With

Left: Wellington of 612 Squadron identical to the one flown by Jeff Rounce on that night in January 1945.
Right: Leading Aircraftwoman Ivy Cross and the citation of her award.

ammunition and flares exploding in the flames, somehow Ivy managed to drag some of the crew away from the burning wreckage. The heat was so intense, she was unable to rescue four of the airmen. That surely would have been sufficient for one night, but as cruel fate would have it, Ivy was not done yet.

Only a few hours later, at 05:00hrs, Wellington '8W-A' of 612 Squadron was on approach. Earlier that evening, it had been out on patrol and had encountered a flotilla of enemy E-boats that, on seeing it, scattered and opened fire on the bomber. They returned home probably having sustained some damage. Chance turned against them even further as the weather by this time had deteriorated so seriously that the cloud base had descended to ground level. In zero visibility and unable to get his bearings, the pilot inevitably crashed his Wellington on landing.

Once again Ivy was alert to the situation and on the scene in no time helping the crew get out of their badly damaged aircraft. This time, thankfully, all survived. For her decisive and courageous actions, she was awarded the British Empire Medal.

The village itself did not escape unscathed. Two villagers and a WAAF all had a very close brush with death on the night of 11th May, 1945. Late that evening, Wellington 'LP404' of No 24 Operational Training Unit based at RAF Honeybourne in Worcestershire was flying a nighttime exercise. Crewed entirely by Canadians, they were engaged in what should have been a routine navigation and bombing training mission over the North Sea. It turned out to be far from routine.

Heading out to the nominated 'bombing' site at 15,000 feet, the young trainee pilot, Flying Officer Maurice 'Maury' East took one of his occasional glances at the gauges, just as he had done throughout the flight according to required regulation for Wellington pilots. To his dismay, he noticed that the oil pressure on the starboard engine had dropped dangerously low. Although still relatively inexperienced, he kept his

calm, immediately shut down the engine and feathered the propeller blades. At first, the crew, confident that their trusty Wellington would get them back home even on one engine, simply made back for Honeybourne, but after a while, Maury could see they were not maintaining decent enough height. They weren't going to make it. He turned to the navigator, Flight Lieutenant Jordan Allen, asking him to locate the nearest base for an emergency landing. Meanwhile, he started dumping excess fuel to help maintain altitude. Eventually "RAF Langham" came the navigator's reply. Taking the new course setting from Jordan, Maury steadily manoeuvred the ailing Wellington and headed for North Norfolk.

By now it was well past 11:00 pm and the sun had long since set. Drawing near to this unfamiliar airfield in the dark with no landmarks to guide him, he began his landing procedure. As he approached the ground, Maury suddenly noticed he was going across the runway instead of along it. He quickly pushed the throttle on the remaining good engine and went round again for a second attempt. This time his luck was out. In manoeuvring the aircraft for another approach, he was unable to keep its height. Realising they were going to crash, Maury concentrated on keeping the Wellington level to minimise the impact. But in the dark, he was completely unaware that the aircraft was heading straight toward the village.

First, they hit some electricity cables putting the lights out across the local area. Then the starboard wing crashed into the roof of one of the village houses. The force of that impact was so great, it spun the aircraft on its axis. As it swung round, the rear of the plane hit a barn, then piled into the YMCA building with the Wellington eventually coming to rest within a few metres of some WAAF barracks. The crash woke the WAAFs inside with an almighty start but they soon pulled themselves together, rushed out and, still in their night clothes, helped the crew get clear of the crash site.

The Wellington was a complete wreck. There was no part of the aeroplane that wasn't ripped to pieces – the nose of the aircraft was missing, the cockpit was smashed up, the port wing was broken in half and had left a gaping hole in the fuselage. Not much of the starboard wing was left, the rest of it was embedded in the house roof and after hitting the barn, the entire tail of the Wellington had come away during the crash. The battered plane lay there smouldering but amazingly did not catch fire which undoubtedly saved the crew, who were now mustering together, wounded and bruised, surveying the wreck and considering their luck.

So too were a few others. Only one hour earlier the YMCA building had been full of WAAF and RAF personnel socialising. Mr & Mrs Sexton had been fast asleep at 1 The Green, when the Wellington's starboard wing had crashed into the roof of their house. Mrs Sexton was bed-ridden and slept downstairs but, as chance would have it, that night, her husband, Frederick, had not felt well himself so decided he too would sleep downstairs with his wife. They escaped with only minor injuries. More miraculous yet was the escape WAAF Verity Gelder managed. Earlier, she had snuck out of the barracks to meet up her boyfriend in the early hours at the village. She had been making her way back to the barracks and was just about to crawl through the perimeter fence when the Wellington came hurtling toward her having taken most of the roof of the Sexton's house and partly demolished the YMCA. Instinctively she dropped to the ground and hoped for the best. It clearly worked because the aircraft came down right beside her with the tail section ending up just above her head. She scrambled out completely – and amazingly – uninjured. The photos on pages 96/97 were from Verity. She had written on the back of one "God is good".

As the crew gathered their thoughts in the aftermath, whilst being tended to by the 'Angels in Pyjamas', the realisation grew that they were missing one of their company, rear gunner Flying Officer Glen Hay. A couple of hours later the rear gun turret was found in the loft of the YMCA building. He was dead. Perhaps if the rear end hadn't collided with the YMCA building he may have survived but if that had been the case and with no damage to the tail, Verity Gerder might have been killed. The remaining Canadian crew were all injured but

Mr & Mrs Sexton's roof is in the centre and the damaged YMCA building is to the right.

The building to the right is one of the WAAF Barracks. Verity Gelder was under the tail section next to the tree.

survived. Hay's death was all the more poignant as it was only three days earlier that the war in Europe had ended.

With the war in Europe over, strategic military locations of Germany fell under the control of the Allies. At the end of July 1945, the Station Commander was posted as Commanding Officer of a captured German airstrip, B151, later renamed RAF Bückeburg. It was being developed into the headquarters of BAFO (British Air Forces of Occupation) and under the command of a familiar face, none other than Air Marshal Sir William Sholto Douglas – the former Air Officer Commander in Chief, Coastal Command. From his visits to Langham, Sir William had obviously been impressed with Clouston and the time had come for the Group Captain to move on and move up. His successor was yet another truly exceptional RAF Officer.

The son of a clergyman, Group Captain Brian E. Paddon, DSO joined the RAF as early as 1929. On 6th June 1940 while

Above: Flying Officer Glen Hay.

serving with 40 Squadron, he was shot down flying a Bristol Blenheim light bomber during an attack at St-Valery as part of the Battle of France. He was captured and became a Prisoner of War. From that moment on he made it his business to escape.

After passing through the interrogation and transit camp of Dulag Luft, he was first sent to Spangenberg and shortly afterwards left for Stalag Luft I at Barth, arriving there on 12th July 1940, where he became the Senior British Officer. Over the next year he made no less than ten escape attempts from various camps. As with other persistent escapees, he was eventually sent to the infamous Colditz Castle on 14th May 1941 along with three other repeat offenders[22].

Not content to be locked up in this notoriously 'impossible-to-escape' prison, he set about doing just that. Given his previous record, escaping from the inescapable was a challenge he was never going to turn down. Eventually, after several thwarted attempts, his best opening arose somewhat by accident. On 11th June 1942 he was dispatched to face a court-martial trial for insulting a German officer following his most recent foiled escape. Whilst awaiting trial, with the help of some other inmates, he took a chance and managed to attach himself to a work party of prisoners that had been allocated to work on a German-occupied Polish farm near Toruń. In another daring move when they arrived at the work site, he slipped into a barn where he stripped off his battledress for other clothes which he had somehow been able to secure with the aid of the other British PoWs. Although the party was under guard, with his next audacious step, he succeeded in nonchalantly walking off as a 'civilian'! From there he meandered his way into the nearby woods and darted for cover. He watched and waited.

When the POW work party left – apparently not noticing his absence – and with the coast now clear, he made his way on foot some 50 kilometres from his point of escape and slipped aboard a train for Bydgoszcz. There he got on another train to Gdynia by way of Danzig (now Gdańsk). He made his way to the city's seaport searching for a ready escape route, but found no sign of the conditions he'd hoped for. He returned to Danzig. It was now the 12th June.

He boarded a tram for Danzig's harbour and spent some time reconnoitring the Swedish ships in the vicinity which were unloading ore. Just before midnight, he crawled down to the quayside through the marshalling yard. He boarded a Swedish ship, the *SS Ingolf*, and succeeded in finding a hiding place on board. He discovered the ship could not set sail for another three days, so he hid in the coal bunker and had to keep himself in the shadow and dodging the falling coal. Before the ship sailed it was subjected to a routine search, but Paddon miraculously remained undiscovered.

Shortly after the ship sailed for neutral Sweden, he revealed himself as an escaped prisoner of war. At first the captain made to turn the ship about and head back to Germany, but Paddon managed to appeal to him to maintain his course for Sweden. The captain eventually acceded on one condition – Paddon was to act as though he were of Polish nationality. Although he knew only a smattering of the language, he readily agreed and was even able to keep up this deception until the ship docked three days later at Gavle, situated on the east coast of Sweden about 100 miles north of Stockholm.

Once the ship docked, Paddon was handed over to the police. Maintaining his agreement with the captain, he duly represented himself as a Polish civilian. In that case, he was told, he must return to Germany. Not to be frustrated again, Paddon quickly declared his true identity and asked to see the British Consul. He was detained in police cells and treated well until, finally, on 27th June, the British Consul visited him. He remained in Sweden whilst his repatriation arrangements were concluded and, on 6th August 1942, at long last he returned to the United Kingdom. He was awarded the Distinguished Service Order and promoted to Group Captain.

This was the imposing man that assumed command on 1st August 1945 after Clouston had left on 23rd July.

The war may have been over, but Paddon did not allow discipline to slip. On one occasion, a weekend shindig was in full swing in one of the hangars and he went to join in the revelry. He left his hat in the entrance, but when he later went to retrieve it, someone had pinched it, presumably as a souvenir. He quickly lost patience and declared angrily that, if it wasn't found and returned to him immediately, he would close the entire function and dismiss the band. A short time passed. The cap was not returned. The assembled throng waited with baited breath. Wholey unimpressed, Paddon unceremoniously ordered the whole affair to be brought to an abrupt end with everyone told to return to their quarters. Having outwitted the Germans in the way he did, his officers and men should not have been surprised in finding him anything other than a man not to be trifled with.

Paddon stayed in charge at Langham for five months until he was posted to 16 Group HQ on the 28th January 1946. The fate of his cap, however, remained a mystery.

As it wound down from its war footing, RAF Langham saw various squadrons inhabiting the now much quieter environs of North Norfolk. These were largely meteorological flights serving alongside 521 Squadron which still resided there. With so many service personnel returning to their civilian lives, the station ceased flying operations a few months later in May 1946.

The country now faced the difficulties of rebuilding. RAF Langham was about to open its doors to more overseas visitors.

8. The Post-War Years: 1946-1958

The war had taken a huge toll on the country. Britain had not only drained its reserves to pay for the war effort but borrowed huge sums of money largely from the US and Canada. So, as life began to return to some measure of normality and the armed forces demobilised, rationing remained and food and raw materials were imported, again under loans now labelled as 'reconstruction'. Gradually though the country got back on its feet.

By contrast, much of Europe was in ruins, some areas literally. A few German cities such as Dresden and Essen were largely reduced to rubble. During the Allied operation to liberate the occupied countries from German control, much of those countries' infrastructure suffered extensive devastation.

The Netherlands was one such country. Consequently, it had neither sufficient financial nor technical resource to support the military training required to re-establish its armed forces. In co-operation with the RAF, the Royal Netherlands Air Force Technical Training School was invited to the UK to take advantage of the facilities here. Langham, with its now semi-redundant accommodation, offered just the place for a technical-military training school to be set up. In June 1946, several hundred Dutch servicemen landed in the village to take over the Nissan hut accommodation evacuated by the

RAF personnel some months previously.

The staff and instructors were Dutch personnel, who had served during the war in the RAF as well as recruits who had joined up having been liberated in 1944 and subsequently gone through a technical training instructor's course at RAF Cosford. There were, also, some RAF officers and NCOs to give further advice. The trainees, who came directly from the Netherlands, were war volunteers and conscripts from the Dutch Navy and Air Force.

Conditions were decidedly uncomfortable and, with one of the most severe winters to come, would get a lot worse. From January to March 1947, there was extensive snowfall. The village was often cut off and the Dutch men found themselves digging the village out. The arrival of spring offered some welcome respite.

Despite the arduous winter, the Dutch trainees were quite well contented with life in North Norfolk. Now that war was behind them and their country was free of occupation, the chance to enjoy working on the rebuilding of their country must have been very welcome. One of the trainees, Jan Stompedissel Menting regularly wrote home to his family. His letters tell a cheery story of his day-to-day life in Langham, his occasional excursions and his memories of the homeland. In April 1947, he wrote to his mother, brother and two sisters back in Amsterdam:

"I stayed home at Easter. Saturday before Easter I went with a few others to Norwich. I had my picture taken there so next Saturday I will have to go there again to pick it up. If the picture is ok, I will have them make an enlargement which I will send over then. Everything is going well here. There is a somewhat nervous atmosphere in the hut tonight, as there are exams on the base tomorrow, and everybody is learning. There also was a fair in Norwich but the coziness of a Dutch fair with its pickles and ice cream stands is missing here. But, it was quite do-able. Have you received my registered envelope yet? From the other one I sent I've already received the confirmation. As I'm writing this I am sitting on my bed, as there's no more room at the table.

I finished my first assignment, I earned 64 points with that. I'm having a good time at the course. It's easy to follow.

The course itself is actually made for people that have had no technical training at all. I find it not at all difficult. That's all I can think of to write, so till next time. Greetings and all the best from Jan"

(Translated by his son from the handwritten letter in Dutch)

Jan's son, Joey, said that his father often spoke fondly of his time in Langham. Some of the Dutch servicemen even found love here and a few went as far as marrying their Norfolk girlfriends, so the time here was not only memorable but also changed their lives. Many years later, in 1997, a party of 80 ex-

service personnel made the journey back from The Netherlands to mark the 50th anniversary of their stay in Langham. A formal reception in the village church was held, a plaque dedicated, and much merriment was had in the Blue Bell!

In the years that followed the Dutch contingent in 1947, a succession of varied units took up the reins at Langham. Mostly, these units continued the enduring association with anti-aircraft training.

43rd Light Anti-Aircraft/Searchlight Regiment, Royal Artillery

The Regiment arrived at Langham in late 1947. The officers were billeted beside Langham Hall, but they had to walk to the camp down the Morston Road to their Mess for meals. The men's huts were dotted around the village in the old RAF camp sites.

They were equipped with 40mm Bofors guns and regularly trained in the Dome. They would then go to Stiffkey for live firing against targets towed by various target tug aircraft in much the same way the target tugs that were the first aircraft to fly out of Langham in 1941. The base had come back to its first roots. The Regiment left in March 1949.

Left: Dutch servicemen clearing snow on the road near the Dome.

No 2 CAACU (Civilian Anti-Aircraft Co-Operation Unit)

This unit, operated by Marshalls of Cambridge on a government contract, was formed during 1951 to take over Army Co-Operation duties in the Norfolk area from No 34 Squadron, which was disbanded at Horsham St Faith just north of Norwich. The unit was initially based not far away at Little Snoring but before too long it was moved to Langham. So once again the base had come full circle with a variety of aircraft operated by the unit performing target tug duties (which was its main role) for a second time supporting the heavy Ack-Ack range at Weybourne and the light gunnery range on nearby Stiffkey marshes.

It wasn't all target tug slog. The unit also had a range of other duties to spice up their lives. Spitfires flew sorties for Army gun laying, Army close air ground support and RAF Radar calibration. A fleet of de Havilland Vampires were added later to supplement the Spitfires. They would often be seen by the local North Norfolk residents flying in line astern, making mock low-level attacks on troops at Weybourne, Kelling Heath, Plumstead Heath and Hempstead Woods. In addition, the unit undertook night searchlight exercises flying Airspeed Oxfords to add to the excitement. The personnel of No2 CAACU were civilian but nearly all had served in the RAF – in fact all pilots had to be members of the RAF Reserve or Auxiliary Air Force. The manager was Jeff Barclay, himself an ex-RAF Flight Lieutenant pilot who had joined up in the first month of the war and served with various squadrons throughout. Jeff's son, Karl, still remembers those days:

"We lived in Blakeney at the time, and I visited the airfield regularly with my father, being allowed to climb in and out of the Mosquitos, Spitfires and other aircraft, and watching the Vampires take off and land. I remember being shown round the Dome when it was being used temporarily to store wing-mounted machine guns to be fitted to RAF Spitfires that came in for servicing.

I got to know a number of the pilots including Veronica Volkersz, whom I remember well as the only woman pilot at Langham towing drogues for Weybourne and Stiffkey anti-aircraft gunners."

As Karl mentioned, one of the most exceptional pilots was a dashing blonde ex-beauty queen by the name of Veronica Volkersz. By all accounts she was a truly gifted flyer and her flying experience extended from pre-war and continued during the war as a ferry pilot with the ATA[23], during which

Right: Jeff Barclay, manager of No2 CAACU, in his Spitfire.

time she delivered hundreds of aircraft of various types that numbered in the dozens. In fact she was the first woman to fly a jet-powered RAF aircraft – a Gloster Meteor in late 1945. It was almost another 50 years before another woman flew an RAF jet.

Sometimes the CAACU aircraft were called upon to take part in ROC and RAF air defence exercises. Defending jets were often surprised when their foe turned out to be a Second World War Spitfire flown expertly by the blonde-haired Veronica!

Another pilot recalled by Karl was Richard Younghusband. He had served in the Second World War with the ATA as a RAF Reserve Officer. Just prior to the war on 25th August 1938, he suffered a terrible flying accident and lost one of his legs and presumably why he went on the reserve list, yet this clearly didn't stop him from flying. After the war he joined Marshalls and ended up with No2 CAACU at Langham. On 23rd July 1953, he was out on a gunnery training flight from Langham in TB747, a Spitfire XVI. At some point in the flight, when attempting to recover from a dive, his aeroplane hit the ground. The doctor and a medical orderly dashed to the scene but were unable to save the stricken pilot.

Karl recollected *"the sad death of Richard Younghusband. I remember my father telling me about Richard's accident at the time, and the effect it had on him."*

Richard Younghusband was the last man to lose his life while

serving at Langham. The Langham Dome Museum has a commemorative plaque in his name in front of the Spitfire on display which is dedicated to him and all others that served at Langham and did not survive.

On occasion pilots and aircraft from the CAACU took part in the making of films. Vampires from Langham appeared in the 1954 film *Conflict of Wings* starring John Gregson and Muriel Pavlow, which featured a storyline about the tension between the rural idyll of Norfolk and fast jets training overhead. Some themes really do stand the test of time!

Despite its contemporary theme, *Conflict of Wings* is not a film that appears on many film buffs' list of all-time greats. However, another film that came to Langham in this period certainly does – *The Dam Busters*. Local boy and volunteer at The Dome, Ian Jarvis, well remembers watching filming taking place on the airfield.

"As kids growing up in Langham in the 50s, the airfield was our playground. We could get into a lot of the buildings, but, even better, we could climb up on top of the roofs. The Guardroom had a big flat roof and we watched from up there as the Lancasters were being filmed as they flew low over the airfield. Obviously we didn't know what it was they were filming. We just excited at watching these great big bombers flying low and loud right in front of our eyes. It was quite a sight!"

During 1958 the training of A-A personnel was coming to an end and the development of surface-to-air missiles for future air defence was well advanced. Together this meant the end for A-A practice camps like Weybourne and Stiffkey and ultimately spelled the demise of No2 CAACU. The last Army co-op flight by the unit was made on 13th October 1958 and, after an air defence exercise a few days later, the unit was closed down.

From 1951 to 1957 there were a considerable number of American army personnel stationed at Langham.
The first unit to arrive was the US Army 50th Radio Controlled

Above: Veronica Volkersz. **Far right:** *Members of No2 CAACU - Richard Younghusband is in the white shirt.*

Gate to Site No 5 as occupied by US Army – the top of the second Dome can just be seen.

Entrance to Site No5 as it looks today – this photo taken from the same spot as the one opposite.

Target Aircraft Detachment. This unit was equipped with large radio-controlled model aircraft. They would launch these aircraft from a circular runway commonly referred to as the 'whirlygig', the remnants of which can be found on the edge of the marsh at Stiffkey. Alternatively, they were launched by catapult from Weybourne. Gunners would attempt to shoot the targets down and, where they failed, the aircraft were recovered by the deployment of a parachute.

In 1953, a Battalion of the 32nd Anti-Aircraft Artillery Brigade arrived. They were equipped with the Skysweeper 75mm automatic radar-operated anti-aircraft gun, fired for the first time in Europe, at Weybourne in August 1954. Personnel for this unit were billeted on Site No 5 on the east side of the Morston Road. For training, the Battalion erected a second dome on the Site No5.

Within this Battalion there was a meteorological section that deployed hydrogen filled balloons from Weybourne. These balloons measured the wind speed at high altitudes, as well as humidity and temperatures, all of which could affect the flight of the shells from the Skysweeper guns. The information was fed into a computer and the gun then adjusted accordingly.

Between 1959 and 1961 the base was used by the British Army Stores Unit while the runways were designated as emergency landing runway for the USAF bombers based at Sculthorpe. That brought RAF Langham's time to a close and it was never used again by military services. The entire site was sold to the Bernard Matthews company who still owns it today.

So Langham's time had been and gone. Now it returned to being a quiet rural stretch of North Norfolk backwater. Despite its remote location, it had witnessed extraordinary things in its active years. RAF Langham, its aircraft and personnel, both air and ground, contributed in no small part to the restoration and maintenance of peace in Europe. The Dome Museum now stands as a unique tribute to their lasting legacy.

Right: Vampire of No2 CAACU at Langham being readied for take off.

Afterword

While researching this modest book, we have seen a multitude of pictures that have struck us deeply – many appearing in the pages above. Images of smiling faces looking straight back at you, not realising the dreadful fate that would lie in wait so closely before them. We have heard, read and witnessed (yes, some of them told by the people themselves) many moving and inspiring stories in the course of our work. As indicated in the Preface, we have tried to make narrative the heartbeat of the book. Indeed, we believe personal stories are at the centre of our museum and the Dome experience.

For those of us that work at Langham Dome, we naturally take great pride in the heritage exhibited to our visitors. But the one thing that stands out to the vast majority of those who come through the door for the first time is those personal histories. Bravery, tragedy, trauma, camaraderie – they are all there.

Our motto *Small Building, Big Story* is not just a facile slogan. So often we see visitors, young and old, initially arrive for the most part with what can be termed as a modest degree of interest – probably subliminally suggested by what they see from outside, a small odd-shaped concrete construction. The diminutive dimensions of the building set in a quiet backwater raises only restrained expectations. And what lies inside is likely to be of similar diminutive scope. But, as they leave an hour or two later, having seen the museum's unique legacy and heard some of the extraordinary heart-warming – as well as heart-wrenching – stories, they enthuse and wonder at the scope and drama of what they found inside.

With news-on-location piped directly into our homes and the all-pervasive internet, these days we are increasingly aware of the harrowing effects of battle, post-traumatic stress disorder and the mental anguish some veterans can suffer. In the years that Langham was an active base there was little such recognition. The label of 'LMF' – lack of moral fibre – was often applied to those whose endurance of repeated appalling experiences had so taken its toll as to render their mental state deteriorated to the point of being unable to function properly. In our minds as Archivists at the Dome Museum, this proves these stories to be even more profound, moving and worthy of preservation.

We have both often said to each other, as we drive along the road approaching the Dome, looking across the now quiet fields to what remains of the runways, that it is difficult not to cast our minds back to a time when the air would throbbing with the sound of Beaufighters or Wellingtons taxiing along the runway to join the aircraft already in the sky heading off on yet another terrifying, nerve-jangling and perilous sortie.

It is equally difficult not to think about what trepidation

the aircrews must have been feeling as they faced the prospect of yet more combat. And what must be going through the minds of those on the ground watching them leave whilst trying not have their thoughts linger on which of their colleagues and friends they weren't going to see again. Spare a thought too, for those who trained in the Dome and then went on to crew the A-A batteries and installations, steadfastly defending against a faceless enemy in the air, surrounded with all the noise, intensity and terror of a fierce air attack – day after day, night after night.

So if you come to our sleepy little corner of North Norfolk – and we sincerely hope you will – do take a moment as you approach The Dome to imagine the skies filling with planes heading off into the distance and think of those brave young souls who put themselves in harm's way time and again, knowing only too well what nightmare they were hurtling toward and yet still had the courage to continue. And in particular, to those that went and didn't come back.

Perhaps fittingly, the last word should rest with someone who was there:

'During the war we were all fighting for our lives and freedom. We were taught to hate. It is a long time ago and we should never hate... I have been to Dachau and felt the horror of what it once was and was touched by the stillness of it as it now is. I have grieved over the suffering that came to so many people. I have met and become friendly with German people, and they are a mixed bag just the same as we are. We must look at home and try to stamp out all the dreadful things which are happening in our own country now. I believe it begins in the home, a loving home which also has discipline.'
Enid Gosney

Above: Enid Gosney, a Langham resident.

Footnotes

1. The company was first established in 1832 by Dr Henry Stephens and expanded overseas with offices as far afield as Australia and New Zealand. Their ink was used to sign the Treaty of Versailles. The company operated until the 1960s when it was bought out by the Equity Corporation of Delaware, USA but the product name remained. Doctor Stephens's son Henry Charles Stephens, known as 'Inky Stephens', inherited the company on the death of his father in 1864.

2. The question of the correct construction date remained unresolved at the time of writing this book. During restoration work carried out on Langham's Dome around 2010, a particular area of internal concrete exposed by the works, was found to be inscribed with a name and date. The name is not clear, but the date appears to be June 1942. Prior to this discovery, received wisdom held quite reasonably, that the Dome was most likely to have been constructed during 1943, a time consistent with RAF Langham's upgrade works, as described in Part II, chapter 5.

3. The Spanish Civil War, fought between General Franco's right-wing Nationalists and the Republicans led by Manuel Azaña Díaz in support of the existing leftist government, lasted from 1936 to early 1939. It was particularly important in this period as the Nationalists were supported by Mussolini's fascist regime in Italy and Nazi Germany. Hitler not only provided military hardware but actually sent his armed forces to participate in the conflict. As a result, the German officers and men, having gained this combat experience, formed a well-practiced and proficient fighting force in the build-up to the Second World War and beyond.

4. The increased flying activity (particularly training-related) experienced after the outbreak of the Second World War, imposed heightened pressure on existing RAF airfields. Consequently, Relief Landing Grounds (RLGs) sometimes referred to as satellite landing grounds (SLGs) were established, mostly in proximity to 'parent' RAF stations. These landing grounds were essentially flat tracts of land providing 1,000-yard grass landing strips, designed, where possible, to blend in with natural surroundings and help conceal the presence of aircraft. Poor drainage was a common problem with RLGs, and they gradually gave way to the more permanent satellite airfields.

5. Docking was chosen as a satellite for Bircham Newton in late 1939. Situated just over 2 miles north-west, the land

(originally Sunderland Farm) offered a large, flat expanse of grass, sufficient to accommodate three runways and associated infrastructure.

6. Inactive at first, operational use finally came to Bircham Newton in May 1918 when, as a training station, it saw the formation of No.3 Fighting School of the Royal Flying Corps. A whole range of aircraft were seen at Bircham in the 1920s and 30s. In addition to military flying, public air displays featured as an annual event in the 1930s and, from 1936, proximity to Sandringham meant that Bircham soon became no stranger to aircraft of the newly formed King's Flight in the years up to the Second World War.

7. Up to the mid-1930s, the RAF was still seen as a minor third service to the more dominant Army and Royal Navy. In 1934, however, Ramsay MacDonald's government announced an increase in the RAF by 41 squadrons. In response to Germany's military expansion this was further increased in 1935. As the threat from Germany escalated, in 1936, a reorganisation of RAF command saw the creation of Fighter Command, Bomber Command and Coastal Command.

8. In all, 63 RAF bombers, including the four 300 Squadron Wellingtons, took part in the raid of 23-24th March 1941.

There were no losses, although the two Wellingtons that crashed on take-off at Langham were eventually written off.

9. After the Africa campaign, he commanded the German forces opposing the Allied cross-channel invasion of Normandy in June 1944. Rommel was implicated in the 20th July plot to assassinate Hitler. Because of Rommel's status as a national hero, Hitler chose to eliminate him quietly instead of immediately executing him, as many other plotters were. Rommel was given a choice between committing suicide or facing a trial resulting in his disgrace and execution. He chose the former and took his own life with a cyanide pill.

10. Despite its outdated appearance, the Swordfish saw a great deal of action in the Second World War including a key role in the sinking of the notorious battleship and pride of the German Navy, *Bismark*.

11. The name originated from a statement by made a German Foreign Office official on 24th April 1942: "We shall go out and bomb every building in Britain marked with three stars in the Baedeker Guide", which was a widely used contemporary travel guide.

12. It was a reputation that came to cause a degree of conflict

and division amongst the senior figures of the Supreme Headquarters Allied Powers Europe.

13. As we now know, Eisenhower postponed the invasion forces departure at the last-minute owing to bad weather in the English Channel. D-Day took place on 6th June 1944.

14. The operations Log reads that the station is to participate in Operation 'Overjoyed'. At first sight, this appears to be a typing error for 'Overlord' but in fact it was a parallel operation led by none other than Air Vice Marshal Hopps, AOC No. 16 Group RAF Coastal Command. The operation was established to search and destroy any German small naval craft attempting to attack the invasion force's naval elements in the period before, during and after the Normandy landings and ran from April to July 1944.

15. As an indication of the time usually taken in pre-flight for example, the navigator on a Beaufighter would typically take on board and prepare the following: signals books, a camera, a pair of binoculars, a flight chart, a flight log, a parachute with an inflatable dinghy, a Very pistol (flare gun) with a set of cartridges and a homing pigeon in a cardboard cage.

16. p23 *Strike and Strike Again*

17. At the speeds of a full powered dive, this required split second precision. It didn't always go to plan – one crew crash landed back at Langham with 3ft of mast embedded in the nose of their Beaufighter!

18. As the vessels being attacked were under steam and the torpedo would be dropped at a range of around 1,000 yards, the pilots had to 'aim off' ahead of the target craft by approximately two ship lengths depending on the speed of the vessel. There was a torpedo sight fitted to *Torbeaus* but the more experienced pilots often relied on their judgement.

19. The rubber dinghies that ditched crews had with them were only intended for short occupancy and, having no power, were at the mercy of the wind and tide. Once a crew was sighted by rescue aircraft, lifeboats with sails and small motors were dropped by parachutes from specially adapted aircraft giving the crews a better chance of getting closer to home where a rescue launch could pick them up.

20. Like Langham, there was also a Dome Trainer to be found at Limavady.

21. Early night operations with the new ASV radar hit upon a problem when the distance between the aircraft and

the target vessel hit the radar's minimum range of about 1 kilometre (0.62 miles). This meant that in the dark, the target was invisible when it disappeared off the radar display. Wing Commander Humphrey de Verd Leigh came up with the idea of using a searchlight that would be switched on just when the target was about to disappear off the radar. Jeff Rounce's new posting, 172 Squadron, was formed to continue the development work in using the new Leigh Light together with ASV radar on anti-submarine patrols.

22. One of the three other officers included Airey Neave who was the first officer to escape the Castle. After the war, Neave was elected as a Conservative MP and served for many years but was notoriously killed in a car bomb attack outside the House of Commons in 1979 with the Irish National Liberation Army claiming responsibility.

23. The Air Transport Auxiliary (ATA) was a civilian unit established during the Second World War tasked with ferrying new and repaired replacement aircraft from factories to the front-line RAF units. What was remarkable about the unit was the number of women pilots (166 in total, approximately 10% of all ATA pilots) and they volunteered from across Britain and the Commonwealth – Canada, Australia, New Zealand, South Africa – and United States, the

Netherlands and Poland.

Bibliography and Further Reading

Barrett, Duncan & Shaw, Nuala *The Girls Who Went to War* (Harper Element 2015)

Bowyer, Michael J.F. *Action Stations 1. Military airfields of East Anglia* (Patrick Stephens Ltd. 1979)

Browning, Stephen *Norfolk at War 1939-1945* (Pen & Sword Books Ltd 2018)

Clouston, Arthur E. *The Dangerous Skies* (Cassell & Co Ltd 1954)

Gordon, Ian *Strike and Strike Again* (Banner Books 1995)

Holland, James *Royal Air Force: The Official Story* (Welbeck 2020)

Kershaw, Ian *To Hell and Back: Europe 1914-1949* (Penguin 2016)

Ministry of Information *Roof Over Britain The Official Story of Britain's A-A Defences 1939-1942* (His Majesty's Stationery Office 1943)

Nesbitt, Roy Conyers *The Strike Wings* (William Kimber & Co Ltd 1984)

Phillipson, Frank *Dome Trainers* (Report 1983)

Pitchfork, Graham *Shot Down and in the Drink* (The National Archives 2005)

Pile, General Sir Frederick *ACK-ACK* (George G Harrap & Co Ltd 1949)

Roebuck, John *Wartime and Post-War Holt* (Holt Society 2015)

Russell, Justin *Dome Trainer, New Monks Farm, Lancing, West Sussex*, Historic Buildings Record (Archaeology South-East Report No. 2020157 Version 2 2020)

Stephens, Henry Christian *Private Journal of H.C. Stephens RNVR: The Dome Trainer 1940-1948* (Imperial War Museum Archive)

Storey, Neil R. *Norfolk in the Second World War* (Halsgrove 2010)

Volkersz, Veronica, *The Sky and I* (W. H. Allen 1956)

Young, Douglas *The Dangerous Sea and The Sky* (Avon Books 1994)

Appendices

Appendix 1:   Abbreviations

A-A	Anti-aircraft or Ack-Ack
AACU	Anti-aircraft Cooperation Unit
AFC	Air Force Cross
ANZAC	Australian and New Zealand Army Corps
AOC	Air Officer Commanding
AOC-in-C	Air Officer Commander in Chief
ASVR	Air-to-surface Vessel Radar
BEF	British Expeditionary Force
CAACU	Civilian Anti-aircraft Cooperation Unit
CB	Companion of the Order of the Bath
CO	Commanding Officer
DFC	Distinguished Flying Cross
DSO	Distinguished Service Order
E-Boat	Small German World War II fast attack boat
PAMPA	Code name for a Met Flight mostly performing pre-attack sorties to check weather conditions
RAE	Royal Aircraft Establishment
RHOMBUS	Code for Met flights across the North Sea
RNVR	Royal Navy Volunteer Reservey
THUM	Thermal Upper-air Measurement
V1	German flying bomb or World War II cruise missile, the 'doodlebug'
V2	German guided ballistic missile
WAAF	Women's Auxiliary Air Force

Appendix 2: Dome Trainers' original locations

Domes built to Air Ministry Drawing 73/42. Those with* are still standing.

1. Alness, Invergordon (x 2)
2. Andover
3. Bovingdon
4. Burtonwood
5. Carew Cheriton, Pembroke
6. Castle Bromwich
7. Chipping Warden
8. Church Fenton
9. Detling
10. Douglas
11. Dumfries
12. Errol
13. Fairford
14. Felixstowe
15. Filey
16. Hook
17. Hornchurch
18. Horsham St. Faith, Norwich
19. Kidlington
20. Langham*
21. Lee-on-Solent
22. Limavady*
23. Lindholme
24. Locking, Weston-Super-Mare
25. Long Kesh
26. Longman, Inverness
27. Lulsgate, Bristol
28. Mildenhall*
29. Montrose
30. Pembrey*
31. Penrhos
32. Portreath
33. Shoreham, Brighton*
34. Squires Gate, Blackpool
35. Sywell, Nottingham
36. Tangmere
37. Tatenhill
38. Tempsford
39. Towyn
40. Warmwell
41. Watchet
42. Wellesbourne Mountford
43. West Raynham
44. Westwood, Peterborough
45. Wyton*

Appendix 3: Units based at Langham

The following were the main units to be based at RAF Langham (detachments and short stay units not listed)

Squadron/Unit	Dates	Aircraft	Role
No1 AACU: K & M Flights	Dec 1941 - Nov 1942	Henleys, Tiger Moths, Lysanders and Defiants	Target tugging
280 Squadron	Aug 1942 - Nov 1942	Ansons	Air sea rescue, coastal patrol and reconnaissance
455 Squadron	Apr 1944 - Oct 1944	Beaufighters	Anti-shipping
489 Squadron	Apr 1944 - Oct 1944	Beaufighters	Anti-shipping
521 Met Squadron	Oct 1944 - Jan 1946	Gladiators, Hudsons, Flying Fortresses and Hurricanes	Meteorological reconnaissance
612 Squadron	Dec 1944 - Jul 1945	Wellingtons	Anti-shipping
254 Squadron	Nov 1945 - May 1946	Beaufighters	Anti-shipping
Met Flights 1402, 1561 & 1562	Dec 1945 - Jan 1946	Hurricanes, Spitfires	Meteorological reconnaissance
No2 CAACU	1952-1958	Beaufighters, Oxfords, Mosquitoes, Vampires and Spitfires	Target tugging and simulation